General Ma:
Local Government.
getting the balance right

by

Michael Clarke and John Stewart

General Editors: Michael Clarke and John Stewart

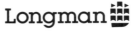

Longman

in association with the Local Government Training Board

Published by Longman Industry and Public Service Management, Longman Group UK Ltd, 6th Floor, Westgate House, The High, Harlow, Essex CM20 1YR, UK.

Telephone Harlow (0279) 442601
Fax (0279) 444501

First published 1990

Printed in Great Britain by Bell and Bain Ltd., Glasgow

British Library Cataloguing in Publication Data
Clarke, Michael
　The management of local government in the 1990's.
　1. England. Local government. Management
　I. Title II.Stewart, John, 1929 Mar. 19-352.0425

ISBN 0–582–06356–6

Summary of Contents

▲ Past traditions of local administration have built an enclosed organisation whose barriers limit the development of both a community orientation and a public service orientation.

▲ Management thus has to open up the authority for the enabling role and to achieve effective service for the public.

▲ Management for the enabling role has its own requirements which are grounded in interaction and community understanding.

▲ Effective service for the public cannot be achieved by those in the field alone; it requires public service management to set conditions for effective service.

4 Challenging the old to build new organisational structures 40

▲ The organisation of the local authority is conditioned by the necessities of what has been required in the past and the assumptions which have grown up around them.

▲ These assumptions have to be challenged if local authorities are satisfactorily to adjust to a new role.

▲ The assumptions support the traditional patterns of working in departments, set within professional boundaries, and structured around hierarchies of control (and, as we shall later explore, of committees).

▲ Once the assumptions have been challenged new forms of organisation can be developed to support the new role.

5 Developing the councillors role for local government 53

▲ The general management of local government requires to be set in a political environment which enhances the changed role of the local authority.

▲ The organisation of the local authority has not supported the full range of councillor roles.

▲ In effect, the committee system has focused the councillors' attention on the day to day working of departments.

▲ The policy and management roles now required are different and challenge the workings of the traditional committee system which provide too little time and space for learning, direction and review.

▲ The representative role of the councillor gains a new importance in the enabling council, but needs to be supported in the working of the authority.

6 Developing changing officer roles 67

▲ As local government changes so change is necessary in the roles required of officers leading to a new management.

▲ The development of this new management cannot be based on the professional role alone but must be about general management.

▲ If general management is to be built for local government then management development must be geared to this end.

▲ Management development must itself be part of a wider approach to human resource management if local authorities are to achieve their full potential as local government.

▲ Management in local government is changing and not just because of legislative change. The external environment and trends in management thinking also have an impact.

▲ Yet the dominance of legislative change and the response to it can create imbalance, building strength but neglecting critical issues.

▲ An emphasis on competitive and contractual arrangements has been promoted by the legislation. It has sharpened management but cannot be all embracing.

▲ A commerical culture is not enough for government. A competitive council has also to be a co-operative council.

▲ The task is to build a new balance in management for local government and for that a holistic approach is required. This is a pre-requisite for general management.

Other titles in the series

Introduction

This book is the eighth book in the management series developed by the Local Government Training Board and published by Longman Group UK Ltd. The series was launched because of the challenge to management in local government posed by government legislation, by a changing environment and by a changing society. Management in local government has to change and is changing as a consequence.

Each of the books published so far has dealt with different aspects of management in local government. Indeed through the books published one can plot the extent and nature of that change. The books have dealt with organisational analysis, with marketing, with human resource management, with the enabling role, with strategic planning, with the changing nature of financial management and with the need to ground management in local authorities on an understanding of the distinctive nature of local government.

In this book we have tried to bring together these and other aspects of management in setting out some of the overall changes that are required if local government is to meet the challenges of the 1990s. We consider that central to this is the need for local authorities to rediscover their role as local government, enabling local communities to meet their needs and problems. This requires a change in the management of local authorities. In the past this has often supported their role as local administration geared to direct provision of services on a continuing pattern.

Change is taking place, but there is a tendency for such changes to emphasise some aspects of management more than others. The book argues for a holistic approach considering not one aspect but the many aspects in their inter-relationship. We describe this holistic approach as *general management* and see it as being needed to guide change. The challenge here is the management of changing more than the management of a once-and-for-all change. For change does not end with the latest piece of legislation or the latest problem that develops in the public arena.

The book itself brings together and adds to material from a series of papers we have written for the Local Government Training Board. We are grateful to colleagues at the Local Government Training Board, at the Institute of Local Government Studies and beyond who have made helpful comments on these papers. We are grateful, too, to the other authors in this series on whose ideas we have drawn. We have both been helped greatly in developing our ideas on management in local government by discussions with officers and councillors from many authorities. We draw upon examples from different local authorities and those examples could be added to by examples from other authorities. Finally we would like to thank Kathy Bonehill at INLOGOV and Enid Orchard at the LGTB for typing many drafts, assembling material and arranging the visits and discussions on which this book is based.

We hope that the book will provide both officers and councillors with a basis to review the management changes required to meet the challenges faced by local government.

Michael Clark, Chief Executive, Local Government Management Board
Professor John Stewart, Institute of Local Government Studies

1 The changing role of the local authority

Key points

▲ *Change is part of the world in which local authorities are set and that change comes not from legislation alone, but from a changing society and a changing environment*

▲ *Change challenges the role that local authorities have come to accept as the administration of direct service provision*

▲ *Change, however, requires from local authorities a rediscovery of local government expressed both in an enabling role and in a new relationship with the communities they serve — role and relationship both needing careful definition*

▲ *If local authorities are to be local government rather than local administration, then management has to change to support the new role.*

The challenge of a changing environment

A changing environment has prompted a great deal of changed practice in the management of local government in the last few years. In part this has been a response to developments in management generally. In greater part, though, it has come as a necessary response to the wider changes taking place in the world within which local government operates. As such it is rooted and grounded in the reality of the issues faced by local authorities.

The environment will change even more fundamentally over the next few years. It is important, therefore, to be clear about what will be demanded of managers and management as that change takes root and we move forward through the 1990s.

Looking at the last few years there have been a series of wide-reaching changes which have had an impact on local authorities. Five stand out:

▽ a deeply changing society and economy to which local authorities have had to respond both in shaping their services and in seeking to guide the development of their local communities

▽ continuing financial restraint, which has limited their capacity to respond to change through growth, and forced reconsideration of past and present activities

▽ declining public acceptance of the form of much governmental action and of imposed professional solutions, which have challenged the certainties of past actions

▽ new and assertive local politics, reflecting the wider changes in society
   and challenging much previously taken for granted in local government
▽ central government programmes which have often struck at the heart
   of the role and ways of working in local authorities.

With so much changing it has been difficult to take stock. There are
some authorities which see all these challenges as a threat. Management in
such authorities has assumed too readily the adequacy of past practices and
sought to continue, unchanged, old ways of working. Change is only
undertaken when it is forced from outside — and then reluctantly. In such
authorities the message is only of decline and of retreat. Morale is low and
managers have seen no opportunities, but only problems.

In most authorities, however, the approach has been different. They
have not labelled each and every challenge as a threat. Past ways of working
do not carry their own justification. Managers have recognised the need for
change — and consciously set out to change rather than merely be changed.
Such management is grounded in acceptance of the reality of change, but
has recognised that there is scope for organisational choice in that reality.
In these authorities there are signs of a new and purposive management
emerging, and it is from this new management that there are lessons for the
future.

Local government in the 1990s is going to be subject to even more dramatic change than was seen in the last decade. Familiar ways of working in
local government have been transformed by a series of legislative measures
including:

▽ compulsory competitive tendering, which has an effect on the working
   of the authority beyond the immediate impact on direct labour organisations. The separation of client and contractor has involved not merely organisational change, but the need to work out new roles. Contract
   management focuses attention on the need for quality assurance.
   Relations between central and service departments are being transformed as newly created direct service organisations make clear their
   requirements, which are expressed in service level agreements. The
   changes inevitably have effects on the whole working of the authority
   requiring dramatic shifts of attitude practice and style on the part of
   managers.
▽ changes in the financing of local government (through the community
   charge and the unified business rate), which maintain or even increase
   the financial pressures under which it operates as well as raising new
   issues about accountability.
▽ in education the introduction of the national curriculum, the local
   management of schools and provision for opting out are transforming
   the role of education authorities and their way of working, making
   them as much concerned with the management of influence as the
   management of action.
▽ in housing the continuing impact of the right to buy, the provisions
   enabling tenants to opt for a landlord other than the local authority, the
   establishment of housing action trusts and the changes in housing
   finance are all leading housing departments to review past ways of
   working.

▽ · the legislation on community care, which means that the local authority has to orchestrate and to regulate a wide range of providers in the public, private and voluntary sectors and that there may well be less emphasis on direct provision in many authorities.

These are not the only changes that have taken place or are proposed in legislation. Changes are also taking place in the control of capital expenditure, in waste disposal separating provision from regulation, in environmental concerns, in the role of local authority companies and in the political structures of councils.

Although some of the changes concern particular services or operations, their combined effects leave few corners of local government untouched. Not least, the role of the local authority will be significantly different, with less emphasis on direct service provision and more on setting the framework within which a range of providers will operate. The legislative changes are however only part of wider changes in the environment, which require local authorities to reconsider their role and their relationships with the public they serve.

The challenge to past roles

These changes challenge the role that local authorities had come to adopt in the long years of growth when it had seemed that the task of local authorities was the administration of growing services based on the accepted professional solution. The tasks of local authorities seemed well defined and clear. The needs were great. Services grew and were assumed to be meeting the needs. They were based on the best professional advice and there was continuing political and public support for the services provided. There was a certainty in the work of the local authority.

The management of local authorities was structured for the stability and uniformity of the established services with committees, departments and professions built around them and the business of the authority defined as delivering them. Stability was ensured by growth, which enabled changes to be met without disturbances to existing services. Uniformity was grounded in professionalism and in the principles of sound administration. The role of local authorities as local administration had its strengths but it meant that local authorities had forgotten their role as local government concerned with the needs of their area and expressing local choice. In the routines of administration the role of local government which provides, the rationale for local authorities, had been lost.

The role of local authorities in direct provision is now challenged by recent legislation and by wider changes in society. The extent and range of the latter changes and parallel changes in public attitudes mean that local authorities are being required to rediscover their role as local government concerned with the problems of their area, beyond the services they provide directly.

There is then both a negative and a positive force leading to a reconsideration of the role of local authorities in the 1990s. The nature of that role will be seen in different ways depending on the emphasis given to those forces. What is clear is that the role can no longer be defined by the services provided alone.

The rediscovery of local government

As local government, local authorities will see their role as concerned with the whole breadth of their community's interests, giving voice to those interests and making or helping make choices about how they should be dealt with. The provision of services will still be important — whether undertaken directly or indirectly — but will be a means to an end, not an end in itself.

Such a reassertion of the role of local authorities as local government is closely related to the continental model of the local authority as the community governing itself, legitimately concerned with all that goes on within it. In a number of European systems this is underpinned by a power of general competence, which allows the local council — subject to suitable safeguards — to take action to meet needs and problems in the community regardless of whether there is specific statutory responsibility. The concerns of the local authority are more than a prescribed set of services, they are the concerns of the community. A full commitment to local government in Britain would be expressed in a power of general competence. Even without that power, however, there are a host of ways in which the local authority can give reality to the new definition of role.

The role of local authorities as local government can be given expression in an *enabling* role. The local authority will be about enabling the community to define and then to meet the needs and problems it faces. It neither requires the direct provision of services or proscribes it. The local authority will act in a wide variety of ways accepting that direct provision of services is one means of providing for the community among many. It will produce some services itself. It will work with and through other organisations — in the public, private and voluntary sectors — aiding, stimulating and guiding their contributions. It will provide the means by which people can meet their needs directly. It will regulate and control, inspect and advise, support and provide grants. It will act within its sphere of statutory responsibility but it will also have a concern for anything which is the concern of local people. It will work to promote the good health of its community. This is the concept presented in this book expressing the role of local authorities as local government.

The enabling council defines its role not by the services it provides but by a broader agenda of concerns. Within those areas of concern it may or

Kirklees prepared with the Friends of the Earth a report on the State of the Environment, setting out the main issues faced and recommending action from whatever organisation was appropriate. 'It is the first attempt in Great Britain to examine, in detail, the major components which make up the environment of a district; and it offers many opportunities for the Council, environmental groups and individuals to identify positive steps to help bring about major improvements in the quality of life'. (Kirklees and Friends of the Earth, 1989) may not directly provide services. The issue of what is required is separated from the issue of how it is to be delivered. Councillors, for example, will still be involved with the interface between services and the community, but they will focus on whether needs are being met rather than on the detailed problems of production. Such a focus need not be a weakening of the local authority. Rather, it is a recognition that its role can be one of *local government*, with concerns for its community which extend beyond service provision.

Once the definition of the role of a local authority in terms of service provided is broken it is easier to conceive this broader concept of local government. For example, the White Paper on Housing argued, as did the Duke of Edinburgh's Housing Inquiry, for the enabling role in housing. A role defined as the local authority having a concern for securing that housing needs are met. That concern is significantly wider than the organisation of local authority housing. The same concept underlies the Griffiths proposals for care in the community now being implemented. These, too, extend the concerns of the authority beyond the service directly provided.

There is, though, a narrower concept of the enabling role reflecting a minimalist view of local government. This would have the local authority doing a lot of the things it does at the present. It must put more and more of its business out to competitive tender, hand over activities voluntarily to third parties or even be required to do so. Residual responsibility will continue to lie with district, metropolitan or county council, but its important job will be to pass on the doing. The local authority would then be about enabling others to act on its behalf providing local services.

There are those who would like to see the present turmoil resolved in favour of the latter definition. This would constrain and fetter and make it difficult for the local authority to be more than a passive intermediary. The challenge to local authorities, therefore, must be to explore and exploit the potential of the broader definition.

Faced with major unemployment North Tyneside 'established an inter-departmental Working Group on Unemployment and set out to undertake an audit of existing services for unemployed people... One of the conclusions we drew from the audit was the necessity to move beyond the phase where the primary objective is generally to promote any activity aimed at unemployed people and into a phase in which developments are based on a clear strategy'. The working party co-opted representatives of voluntary bodies involved in unemployment initiatives. One key element of the stategy has been the creation of local centres in which 'a qualitatively different style of service would be possible within the scope of small locally based facilities that avoid the traditional professional/client style of working and foster work *with* the unemployed as compared with service *for* them. This style of service delivery can incorporate the communities' experience and builds upon these rather than the good ideas of professional staff however committed' (Gallant, 1988).

There are sufficient major discontinuities to ensure that the role of local government will change. How it will be played out as the 1990s progress is an open question. What is urgent is that people in local government recognise the extent of the changes taking place and think and plan anew. Focusing on problems alone may destroy local government from within; but the idea of the enabling council as local government carries with it considerable opportunities if the broader view is taken. Some may feel that the enabling concept is difficult to develop at a time when powers are being reduced; the key question must then be whether the full potential of the local authority has ever been fully realised and whether there is not an opportunity to make progress towards it.

The potential is already there. Much has changed in the last few years and the capacity for innovation and imaginative thinking is well demonstrated. Across the political parties, many elected members have shown both frustration with much of the traditional approach of local government and willingness to experiment and search for new solutions to the problems of their communities. Many managers and professionals have shown similar inclinations and have themselves been quick to look for new models and approaches. Both members and managers need to make sure that the initiative is grasped to give expression to the broader view of what it means to be an enabling council.

Developing the enabling role as government

The enabling council needs to recognise the complex of agencies and organisations which touch upon local communities and those who live within them. It needs to recognise the resources that lie within communities and to develop them. If the resources available are not used to the full on behalf of the community, the local authority will limit its role and weaken its capacity to assist and guide. The council that limits itself to what it can do directly, limits its contribution to the community.

As has been said, the enabling role does not rule out direct provision if that is the most effective way of enabling the community to meet needs and problems. What it does do is to focus attention on how services are best provided and by whom. This means, too, that in the running of services the emphasis must be on the public served. The attention of councillors has to be focused less on the organisation of the service and more on the public as customer and citizen. The enabling role, far from ruling out direct provision, provides a challenge to management to ensure that the provision of services meets needs felt and understood by the community served.

The enabling council will, however, use a variety of other methods and draw on a wide range of resources in the community to meet local needs. Many of these methods already play some part in local government life, but they are becoming more central and more focused. The authority can, for example:

▽   contract work out to another local authority or public sector organisation
▽   contract work out to the private sector
▽   enter into a partnership with other agencies
▽   contract with and/or give grants to voluntary bodies to provide services

Bradford has decided that 'too many services are directly controlled by the Authority. It will be necessary to involve the wider public in determining the nature of council services. The council must allow direct control over many activities to devolve to other forms of community organisation. These may include:

> Public/private partnership (e.g. community trusts)
> Direct user organisations (e.g. school governing bodies or housing co-operatives)
> Private associations (e.g. Housing associations).' (Bradford, 1989)

▽   join with other organisations to create a new agency to provide services
▽   co-operate and consult with organisations

The Mission Statement for Wear Valley District Council states that 'The Council also intends to secure the maximum utilisation and cooperation of all other organisations and resources within the District to make Wear Valley a positive and beautiful place to work, live and visit'. (LGTB, 1989)

▽   use powers to regulate
▽   draw up community plans

Wiltshire County Council is developing a rural strategy to be prepared with 'District Councils and other bodies with an interest in Wiltshire's rural areas, and to contain policies which they would wish to support'. (Wiltshire, 1989)

▽   advise and guide
▽   give grants to individuals
▽   use its statutory powers to assist community initiatives
▽   create forums for discussion of issues
▽   bring people together to stimulate thinking and prompt action
▽   help groups of users or consumers to meet their needs directly
▽   give publicity and campaign on issues of concern.

West Lindsey District Council played an active role as a lobbyist in opposition to the designation of sites for the disposal of radioactive waste. It 'was hoped that the Council's policy would function to engender and draw on widespread public and professional support and serve as a platform for united political opposition'. (Cairns, 1989)

Such methods are discussed in the book entitled *Managing the*

Enabling Authority by Rodney Brooke, published in this series. It is important to recognise and think through the possibilities. There is no point in seeking to establish the enabling role without being clear about the means to enable. If a local authority has identified areas of concern, it must have the means of doing something about them. Thus, an enabling council concerned with housing in its area is impotent unless it has points of leverage with which it can effect the housing position. An enabling council needs powers and resources. It may find some unexpected points of leverage in the powers it already has; the leverage it has got has to be explored, understood and exploited.

If the enabling role is regarded as the expression of the role of the local authority as local government, there are many things which have to change. As local government local authorities should represent the community governing itself. That requires a more active relationship with the community than has often been the case. Equally, as already hinted, it means that where services are provided — either directly or indirectly — the local authority must ensure that services are provided for people and not merely to them. It means that accountability is not merely achieved through a periodic election, but is a continuing process based on an active citizenship. It means that the authority has to listen and to learn.

Current relationships with other agencies and organisations — and the means of facilitating them — may be quite inadequate to support the new role. The relationship between the local authority and its public at large will need to become close. The council will be much more about making choices on the issues faced by the community and planning with and for the community to resolve those issues; helping and guiding many initiatives; using many modes of social action. It will need councillors who can take a lead in this and managers who can deliver.

The new approach required

The real test of any attempt to develop the idea of the enabling council as local government will be how far an authority goes in thinking about its role beyond the services it provides, and of using the means available to make the role effective in practice. This might ultimately come from a new legislative base; in the meantime existing powers and resources have to be used.

The possibilities of renewal from within become clearer when the experience of other countries is looked at. The 'free commune' experiments of Scandinavia and other European countries encourage local authorities to identify regulations and controls which they would like to see lifted in order to allow them to meet the needs of their communities (Stewart and Stoker, 1989). In these experiments councils are being encouraged to take initiatives to help their communities either through direct provision or by enabling others. Official impediments are being removed. In each of the countries concerned, the experiments have stimulated initiative and innovation and many of the proposals made by authorities have not required a change in controls. The local authorities already had the powers they sought, but had assumed too readily they were constrained by statute. The results are instructive for British local government, which has for so long felt constrained at every turn.

The difference is that in those countries there is active encouragement by central government for imaginative thinking and innovative action. Lcoal authorities are being stimulated and empowered to take new initiatives. No such experiment is taking place here. Indeed, many people inside local government are only too aware of new constraints. But opportunities exist; the lesson for UK local government must be to consider the freedom and resources still available and then to think about new ways of using them. There are many individual examples of experiment and initiative, but concerted new thinking from within local government is needed in order to produce renewal.

The first — and perhaps most important — need is to break away from the constraining organisational assumptions that limit a council's role to the direct delivery of services. This is more difficult than it sounds, for the assumptions constrain thought, structure and processes. For officer and member alike there are accepted ways of doing things; for example

▽   a department is structured for direct provision of services. Its hierarchies of control and its procedures naturally focus on direct provision. It behaves as if this were the only approach.
▽   the committee focuses upon the organisation and on day to day operations. It easily becomes more concerned with the organisational exigencies of service delivery than the needs of the community.

These assumptions and their implications are considered further in Chapters 4 and 5.

Once they are broken away from all manner of other things follow. The structure and style of traditional departments may no longer be appropriate. Committees matching these departments and based on particular services may not be able to give the necessary space and coverage to wider community concerns. Political agendas will need to be re-shaped to encompass these wider issues and elected members will need to take on different roles. Such roles will be more challenging for they would reflect the wider concerns of the council. New kinds of professionals and managers will be required if the potential is to be grasped.

Realising the potential

If the potential to develop its role as local government — the enabling role in its widest sense — is to be realised the local authority has to recognise:

▽   that there should be a constant search for gaps and weaknesses in community provision
▽   that the authority should build an active relationship with those who live and work within its area, listening and learning from them
▽   that direct service delivery is not the only response to community needs
▽   that resources available are not limited to those within the authority
▽   that there are many modes of social action and their stimulus and encouragement is a role for local authorities
▽   that the role of the local authority is extended by working with and through others
▽   that the local authority has to look outward to agencies, organisations and individuals

▽ that committee and departmental structures are not sacrosanct and
that new styles and approaches to the business of the council and its
work will be needed.

The incorporation of these elements presents a challenge for members
and officers. Local government does not just happen. The enabling role
must be worked for. In particular it requires management processes,
approaches and styles which extend beyond conventional boundaries and
thinking which is so often conditioned by the existing organisational
assumptions. It requires an understanding that is not limited by traditional
ways of working. The most important of the new requirements are explored
in the chapters which follow.

2 A new management for a changed role

Key points

▲ *The changing role of the local authority requires a reconsideration of its management. Although this has changed significantly in the last decade further radical change is needed*

▲ *There is a need to think of the whole, while building gradually towards a new management which is general management as opposed to professional management*

▲ *The local authority of the 1990s requires a management with clear characteristics. For example, strategy has to be developed, but responsibility must be devolved; political processes must guide action, but responsiveness to customer and citizen is also required. In these and many other ways balance must be sought in a holistic approach.*

The effectively managed authority

The challenges posed to management in local government by its changing role are deep and wide-ranging. The urgent need is to build effective organisations capable of meeting them. To do this the various strands have to be drawn together in a new management.

The attributes which mark out this new management are not separate but reflect inter-related themes in the working of the authority. It is not that they are necessarily new or solely prompted by changed roles; it is rather that taken together they represent a major shift. An effective local authority should:

▽ be close to the citizen and customer
▽ be able to learn from a changing environment and apply that learning
▽ be capable of using that learning to determine strategy and policy direction
▽ work through political processes which steer management action
▽ be guided by organisational values and style
▽ devolve responsibility and sharpen accountability
▽ have an organisational capacity to recognise and deploy a wide range of powers, influence and resources in many different ways
▽ continually review performance
▽ fully develop and use its human resource recognising the importance of equal opportunities
▽ purse new ways of working through organisational innovation.

An holistic approach is required, which enables consideration of not just one aspect of management, but of the inter-relationships and achieving balance within the organisation. It is then not just an holistic approach that is required, but of being able to build towards the whole in a *gradual or piecemeal* way. It is being able to see opportunities — or weaknesses — and being able to act at the appropriate time, with each action contributing directly to building the whole. It is also about being able to use change to good advantage.

There is always a temptation to seek stability in an organisation and to end up responding to change in a reluctant way. We have already shown that the one certainty of the next few years is that there will be large scale change. Managers should seek sufficient stability to give their organisations confidence but, at the same time, encourage them to thrive on the change which is taking place and use it to their advantage. Managing cannot be about being neat and tidy.

These attributes should apply to the whole of management regardless of discipline or service. Hence it is important to talk in terms of general management — rather than professional management which emphasises the differences between services and not the things which unify. General managers in education, social work or environmental health need to be sensitive to the particular concerns of those disciplines but should not allow them to come in the way of the broader view. That is the nature of the new management of local government.

Close to the citizen and customer

The local authority acts on behalf of the whole community. One of the most exciting trends of recent years has been the new emphasis given to the relationship with the public — both as citizens at large and as customers of services. A vigorous local authority will want to build this relationship. It will be as important when services are provided through other organisations, as when they are provided directly. A local authority can easily become an enclosed organisation providing service *to* the public, rather than *for* the public. It looks inward to the organisation rather than outward to the public. It focuses on the procedures it has established rather than on the public it services. Because the authority reckons it knows what the public needs, it does not try to find out what the public wants or thinks or suggests.

Change challenges the enclosed local authority. The public no longer accepts authority actions as justifying themselves. In a changing environment old judgements on patterns of provision are challenged; services no longer carry their own justification. Justification lies in service for the public. The meaning of public service has to be rediscovered from the public served.

The enabling council needs to extend this interest beyond the services it provides directly. Not only will it need to find the means to learn about wider community concerns; it will need to infuse other agencies or organisations with which it works or contracts with the same obsession for putting the public first. It will need to *think public* in all that it does, with a wider frame of reference than simply its own services.

All this requires managers — and members — to think in terms of *marketing*. It has been thought to be the preserve private sector but marketing has major lessons for the local authority although it must be developed to meet the purposes, conditions and tasks of local government. Marketing in local government may be more concerned with discovering need than with stimulating demand. The challenges of *Marketing in Local Government* are discussed by Kieron Walsh in the book in this series. The relationship of the authority with its public both as customer and as citizen is discussed further in Chapter 3 of this book.

The learning organisation

Being close to the customer and citizen demands a capacity to learn, respond and adapt far removed from the traditional bureaucratic organisation designed for stability and continuity. The enabling council needs a capacity for learning that extends the authority's area of concern. The enabling role, if fully developed, will require local authorities to have as wide as possible an understanding of their areas, and of the problems and issues faced and the resources available for meeting them.

Learning must encompass:

▽ the changing environment
▽ changing knowledge
▽ performance and failure as well as success
▽ understanding the impact of the authority's own action
▽ appreciation of the organisation's strengths and weaknesses
▽ other organisations; the way they act, what they do and what they can do
▽ the public and its wishes, needs and judgements.

The traditional learning of local authorities has followed predetermined patterns. A local authority has learnt through procedures geared to a continuity of service provision, through organisational structures formed around existing services and through well-established professional channels. New ways of learning are required if local government is going to break out of well-established patterns. There is no one method for this. It will involve such things as:

▽ experimentation and use of pilot schemes to probe and test possibilities, allowing that mistakes are as important in learning as sucesses
▽ developing environmental analysis which extends organisational understanding of changing external problems

The London Borough of Richmond has made extensive use of surveys to establish the views of users and the public at large on the services provided. It has instituted procedures to ensure that the issues raised are considered by committees and by management. Thus 'raw data from Richmond's opinion survey are presented to the committee involved with rate-setting in February. The full report is sent to all members at the end of March, and an overview paper is prepared for the Policy and Resources Committee. Service chiefs also write papers for their own committees...' (LGTB, 1988)

▽ building inter-organisational understanding so that learning is not limited to the capacity of the local authority

> Hammersmith and Fulham carried out a survey of public attitudes
> towards council services. Before carrying out that survey, panel dis-
> cussions were held to ensure the questions to be raised in the survey
> reflected key issues felt by local people. Special panel discussions with
> specific groups were for example:
>   'elderly women in sheltered accommodation
>   male and female members of an Afro-Caribbean social centre
>   members of an Asian women's group
>   a group of mothers at a one o'clock club
>   members of an organisation for unemployed people
>   members of two centres for people with disabilities'. (LGTB,
>   1988)
> This meant the survey was designed to obtain both general informa-
> tion and information on disadvantaged groups.

▽ the development of output measures and inter-authority comparisons
as a basis for improving performance
▽ the development of qualitative assessment and service impact studies
▽ watching closely the experience of contracted out services
▽ committee procedures which provide space for quality review and performance assessment
▽ staff training and development which extends knowledge and skills and
builds up personal capacity for learning.

But organisational and individual learning by themselves are not adequate. Learning has to be used and must be reinforced by active review, In
the day-to-day working of authorities, attention can easily be focused on
the necessities of immediate action, obscuring the need for review. Space
needs to be protected for review which must not be limited to the isolation
of a performance review committee and which should become second
nature to managers because it is only through review that learning can be
linked to action.

Strategic management and policy direction

The traditional working of local government was built on continuity of
activity. The focus was on the maintenance of existing activities and their
adjustment through incremental growth. The direction was implicit.
Practice and procedures revolved round such apparent certainty and stability. In a changing society a local authority needs a capacity to develop a
community strategy to guide both its own activities and those of other
organisations. Unless special effort is made the day-to-day requirements of
operational management dominate the business of the authority, and existing activities and methods of working maintain their own imperative
leading it to neglect both emerging problems and the role of other organisations. The limitations of the operational perspective can be challenged by
strategic management which:

▽   looks outward to problems and needs: it focuses on key issues not on present activities

▽   searches out the resources within the community: it acts not merely directly but enables individuals and organisations to meet those needs and problems

▽   is selective: direction is not found in detail but in priorities and in the identification of key changes

▽   exposes choice: existing activities conceal the choice that is made and re-made in continuity

▽   is guided by political purpose: it gives direction to the authority

▽   recognises uncertainty: it is concerned more with possibilities than precise prediction

▽   ensures that organisation and people are geared to deliver: it is realistic in terms of achievement.

Strategic management is thus a continuing management process. It is more than just the production of a strategy, although such statements mark stages in the process and give a sense of purpose to those who work within the authority. The process involves analysis both of environmental changes and of organisational strengths and weaknesses. It is informed by political priorities.To be effective it will involve organisational development as well as embracing planning and resource allocation. Strategic management must give purpose to policy and ensure that the organisation can realise that purpose.

Strategy by itself is not enough, however. Associated with it there must be clarity of policy. In a period of change policies cannot merely be left implicit in the activities undertaken. They must be stated to be understood. Understanding is necessary if the organisation and its staff are to realise policy in action. It is all the more necessary where the authority acts through other organisations, either because it chooses or is required to do so. In drawing up contracts under compulsory competitive tendering, or determining the way a voluntary agency will act on its behalf, the local authority has to start with its requirements.

General management must build strategic management and clear policy direction. Experience suggests that its processes can be developed in a variety of ways:

▽   through reviews undertaken of the changing environment

▽   by identifying the key issues facing areas and those who live and work within them

---

Kent County Council has built its own approach to strategic management. 'We have looked at various private sector approaches to strategic management; whilst they help in the thinking, their practical application is limited. The reason is simple. In the private sector the bottom line is performance measured in terms of profit achieved. In County Councils performance is measured against political values and performance achieved. Consequently we are working to a simple concept of strategic management, balancing the 'performance requirement' against 'operational' capability'. (Sabin, 1989)

▽   in the production of strategy documents setting the key directions for
    the authority and for and with other organisations
▽   through drawing up medium-term guidelines setting priorities for
    financial plans beyond the immediate year.
▽   in reviewing services to establish the appropriateness of existing poli-
    cies and sharpen the focus of priorities.

These issues are explored in the book *Planning for Change* by Ian Caulfield
and John Schulz in this series.

Reading Borough Council has prepared a strategy to give itself 'a
clear direction and clear priorities. The overriding theme of the strategy is the tension between the need to provide high quality services in
a changing world whilst having reducing resources. Without a clear
strategy and priorities this tension will drag the council down'.
(Reading, 1985).
The strategy sets out:
▽   the opportunities and challenges facing Reading
▽   The Priority Programme
▽   How to implement the Priority Objectives.

Guided by political processes

Local authorities are political institutions constituted for local choice.
The extent and nature of that choice is constrained by the legislative framework within which local authorities are set, but choice remains. Indeed, the
process of compulsory competitive tendering focuses the attention of the
political process on the choice on what is required.

Local choice is legitimated by local elections, themselves an expression
of a political process. The political process is at the heart of local government. The emerging roles of the council place an emphasis on community
leadership which depends on the political process.

Management must look for ways of building a new mutuality between
the elected members and the officers of the authority. This must encompass their roles and relationships. Management should not become shut off
from the political process because that is what gives it its purpose. Rather it
should support and interlock with the process. In doing so management
cannot assume that past settings and procedures give adequate support to
the process. Changing politics cannot necessarily be contained, for
instance, within the workings of the traditional committee system and the
procedures built for its support.

Management needs to secure political direction which gives purpose to
the organisation in a changing environment. That direction is often best
developed in new settings and procedures which encourage a debate which
is wider and more free than is possible in committee. Such settings allow
both discussion to break out of committee constraints, and recognise
political reality and the need to relate political purpose to management
action. They also assist elected members to develop their role as community leaders for the enabling council. Chapter 5 discusses the issues
involved.

Organisational Values and Management Style

Many managers have learnt that change is better managed by concern for processes and particularly by establishing values and developing style, rather than by simply altering structures. Local authorities have too often pursued the frustration of structural change, instead of recognising that some of the softer aspects of organisational life can be crucial. The processes which underpin the way the organisation works, the assumptions made, its values, and the style of the organisation are usually a more pervasive influence than formal structures. It is this that has led to a concern for the culture of the organisation; a phrase that encompasses assumptions, values and style and is expressed in an organisation's way of working.

Effective management requires as widely shared an organisational understanding of the values as possible. These should inform the organisation's working, and those who work within it. At a time of challenge and change the importance of recognising organisational values grows. A local authority will not achieve closeness to the public simply by modifying procedures, although change in procedures may be necessary where they hinder closeness. Closeness to the public will only be achieved by an organisation in which that is felt — and seen to be — a key value by those who work within it.

There are, and always have been, organisational values in local government. They have usually been implicit and have more often been the fragmented values of departments than those of the authority. The dominant values have been professional, for in each department there has been a dominant profession which has set the way of working and the norms of behaviour.

At a time of change organisational values need to change. The new management, while not denying the role of professional values, will need to build shared organisational values. These will be limited in number and serve to focus rather than to disperse attention. They will be encapsulated in short phrases: public service; closeness to the customer; equality of opportunity; value for money; quality; integrity and respect for the individual; partnership between councillors and employees; bias for action; productivity through people; lean staff — keep it simple.

They can be communicated in many ways: in training, in newsletters,

Bromley London Borough has adopted a Management Style based on:

'Maintain bias for action
Stick to what we are best at; experiment selectively and in small steps
Respect the individual and seek productivity through people
Promote authority and entrepreneurship and recognise the risks
Promulgate clear values and seek active leadership
Keep close to our customers
As we have a lean staff — keep it simple
Keep to the centre only that which is necessary: trust'. (Bromley)

but above all in the actions of senior management. Once asserted, values have to be continuously reinforced by experience to have meaning.

Devolving responsibility and sharpening accountability

One of the most notable trends in all management — far beyond local government — has been the move to pass responsibility down the organisation and, in doing so, to sharpen accountability. Legislation in education, social work and compulsory competitive tendering is leading local authorities to devolved management. The real need arises not from legislation, however, but from the need to create organisational space for effective and responsive management.

Too often in local authorities, hierarchical control and detailed financial and establishment controls have limited management capacity. Detailed control has been substituted for effective management. The emphasis has been on following procedures not on management achievement. Detailed control is only necessary if directions are not clear and policy is not understood. Devolution of responsibility is not the removal of control but the substitution of effective control for detailed control. It depends upon:

▽   a clarity of policy
▽   an understanding of the parameters within which action can be taken
▽   the specification of the targets a manager is expected to achieve
▽   accountability for what is achieved
▽   management information matching responsibility and accountability.

Many of these requirements are necessary for competition and contracting out. They are as important if the service is provided directly as if it is provided through a contract.

The devolution of management responsibility requires reconsideration of the role of central services, both for the authority as a whole and within departments. Managers responsible for their budgets and held accountable for them will not accept unchallenged either the level of overheads or the service received for these overheads. Pressure grows for the right to choose and pay for (or not choose and not pay for) the services provided by the central departments.

The successful experiments in devolving responsibility and sharpening accountability have also led to:

▽   reviewing financial control to allow virement within cost centres
▽   devolved personnel management

> Berkshire County Council is developing devolved management based on cost centres. After a pilot project in 1988, the process has now been extended to 600 cost centres. 'Devolved management is not physical decentralisation although it shares many of the consumer oriented objectives. Devolved management is the maximum delegation of responsibility — authority plus accountability to managers throughout the Authority.' (Geeson and Haward, 1990)

▽   rigorous processes of accountability review
▽   of performance appraisal for managers.

Some of the issues involved in these developments are examined in the
book on *Financial Management in the 1990s* by David Rawlinson and Brian
Tanner in this series.

Deploying powers and resources

The powers and resources available to a local authority are many and
various. The enabling role means that it has to relate them not merely to
services provided directly, but to the wider needs and opportunities identified. It has to learn to use them in new ways: to stimulate, to guide and to
assist as well as to provide.

Before being able to use the powers and resources at its disposal it has
to identify and to understand their potential. Whilst this sounds straightfor-
ward, it involves looking at powers and resources in new ways including:

▽   the information available to the local authority
▽   the intricate network of contacts which it has built up
▽   the land and property it owns
▽   the skills and experience of officers and councillors
▽   the inter-locking system of appointments, which brings councillors and
    officers into the working of many outside organisations
▽   financial resources
▽   access to government or other grants
▽   the power to command attention and speak on behalf of the com-
    munity
▽   the formal or informal standing the council has in the community
▽   powers of inspection, licensing and control
▽   powers to provide services or to contract with others to do so
▽   powers to purchase goods and services
▽   powers of compulsory purchase.

Such an inventory shows the potential powers and resources available
to the council; but the council has to learn to use these instruments to gain
leverage for the enabling role.

The authority cannot restrict its consideration of powers and resources

Tendring District Council has considered how it can develop the
enabling role. 'Local authorities must accept that their role has to be
extended by working with and through others and we need to look to
organisations, agencies and in some cases individuals to achieve that
aim. There will need to be a constant search for shortfall in community provision and for ways in which we can meet and finance that need,
not solely from within the Local Authority' (Bleakley, 1989). It has
decided to make a series of appointments of advisers in a number of
areas (for example grounds maintenance, building maintenance,
European and Cultural affairs) who can assist voluntary bodies, community groups and sports associations to run their own affairs.

within set committee or departmental boundaries, as has been characteristic of so much of traditional working. It needs to be able to take a strategic and corporate view. For example, the enabling role in relation to housing depends upon planning and environmental health powers, as much as upon powers in relation to housing. Both members and officers need to develop new ways of looking at their resources and need an imaginative understanding of how they can be developed. These issues are explored further in Chapter 3 and in the book *Managing the Enabling Authority* by Rodney Brooke in this series.

Reviewing performance

Underlying each of the approaches being developed in the new general management should be a commitment to reviewing performance:

▽   the authority that is close to its citizens and public must discover their views on its performance as they are in the best position to judge
▽   the learning organisation cannot assume that past performance is a guide to future action
▽   strategies defined and policies clarified have to be tested against actual performance
▽   political processes are only fulfilled in the performance achieved
▽   values and style are only words until they have a real impact on performance
▽   responsibility devolved and accountability enforced will only work if performance is reviewed
▽   the development of the human resource is best measured against performance fulfilled
▽   organisational innovation has to be examined in the light of performance achieved.

Performance review is therefore central to general management. It is obviously a required basic discipline of the management of contracts, developed as a result of compulsory competitive tendering but is much wider than this. In a changing environment activity cannot be assumed to justify itself; it can only be justified in the performance which is achieved. Equally, past performance cannot be assumed to be the standard for future performance. Performance must continually be re-defined in a way appropriate to the times.

Performance review has many levels:

▽   the member of staff in individual achievement
▽   the customer in satisfaction
▽   the contract in terms of conditions fulfilled
▽   the service in standards achieved
▽   the authority in policy goals reached
▽   the community in needs met:–

MAKING A LADDER OF PERFORMANCE REVIEW

General management should see performance review as a continuing process and as part of the basic discipline of both management and policy making. Consequently it should not be fragmented in an ad hoc pattern or isolated in a single committee. To be successful it depends on assessment. Assessment, in turn, requires the use both of direct performance measures and indirect indicators of performance. Thus it will combine both quantitative or hard data with qualitative or soft data. It is as important to recognise, seek out and use the latter as it is the former.

Organisational time and space is necessary for review. The pressure of day-to-day events and the difficulty of seeking the means of assessment, together with having to face the problems of weak or poor performance, are all apt to crowd out the opportunity for review. Once the time and space are secured and review conducted, there must be determination to learn from its results and to set new purposes and tasks. This can be done in:

▽ the accountability review of staff performance
▽ the workload review of a section
▽ the contract review of standards reached
▽ the quality review of a service
▽ the review of a department's achievements
▽ the review of an authority's strategy
▽ the review by the community of the local authority's achievements.

Performance review will be further explored in a book in this series by Steve Rogers on performance management.

Hackney London Borough has introduced procedures for Quality of Service Review Assessment which will pose such questions in Committee Reports as:
1 Which client groups/geographical areas are affected by proposals in the report?
2 Do the proposals redistribute services/resources and if so in what ways and between which groups or geographical areas?
3 Are service levels clearly specified?
4 Are clear goals and monitoring arrangements set in relation to activities and targets? (Hackney, 1987)

A VALUED STAFF

An undervalued staff will not provide a valued service. A local authority cannot respond to challenge and changes except by and through staff—even when it is taking action through other organisations. There are four requirements from any authority's staff policies:

▽ to ensure that staff understand the purposes and policies of the authority and what it is trying to achieve
▽ to ensure that the full potential of staff is realised and their experience, knowledge and skills are used to the full
▽ to ensure that staff are helped to develop to meet the challenges and changes faced by local government
▽ that policies and procedures which affect staff reflect the values and vision of the authority.

Too many authorities communicate too little with staff, neither learning from them nor giving them sufficient information for the meaning of their policies to be understood. It cannot simply be assumed that staff understand the policies of the authority. Nor can it be assumed that staff have reached their full potential or that change can be managed without a clear and explicit commitment to staff development. Communication, moreover, is a two-way process. It involves listening to what people have to say as much as it does telling them what is going on.

Human resource policies need to be built from the authority's strategy. To develop staff without a vision of how the organisation is to change is of little value. Staff development must be guided by a sense of organisational purpose and direction. Given that sense of direction as wide a range of opportunities as possible should be used to build a positive approach to staff development.

Underlying a commitment to staff development must be a concern for equal opportunities. Both staff and organisational development is frustrated by discrimination whether intended or unintended. Opportunities need to be provided for women, people from the ethnic minority communities, and the disabled, to progress through the organisation. Discrimination, particularly in recruitment, selection and promotion, needs to be confronted and a constant vigilance maintained to ensure that the organisation is doing more than make symbolic gestures.

Some members and officers argue that there is no problem and that equality of opportunity is woven into the fabric of their organisations. The absence of women and black people, for example, in the ranks of senior management is testament to the shallowness of this argument. There are deep changes taking place in society at large which need to be better represented in the world of local government. There are also differences of style which are associated with difference in cultural background and gender which enrich management.

Developing the full potential of the human resource also means involving everyone in the life of the organisation. More and more managers are discovering that collective performance is greatly improved if staff at all levels are given a full sense of responsibility, encouraged to seek ways of improving the way their bit of the organisation works, and involved as members of teams which can control their pattern of working by achieving clear objectives and targets. Commitment and motivation is also enhanced where staff are listened to and celebrated as key parts of the organisation's life.

The issues involved are discussed in the book in this series by Alan Fowler on *Human Resource Management*, as well as being further explored in Chapter 6.

Organising for a new role

The organisational structures of local authorities have been built to support past ways of working based on the direct provision of services on the established pattern. New ways of working are required which cannot easily be contained within those structures.

▽   the hierarchies of departments built for control of direct service provision may limit the development of community action and of responsive services

▽   working across organisational boundaries requires structures that do not confine action within those boundaries

▽   compulsory competitive tendering requires the separation of client and contractor roles merged in past organisational structures

▽   an entrepreneurial approach required to realise opportunities challenges existing systems and procedures built for the control of established services

▽   learning from the community can easily be lost in departmental tiers or between departmental boundaries.

The requirements of the enabling role challenge the conventional structures and procedures which have been built for the continuing stability of direct service delivery. Organisational boundaries build barriers for the public. What is needed is not a simplification of structures and rules, but a collective attitude of mind which is about innovation and experiment (supporting those who try, whether they succeed or fail) and encourages the search for examples of good practice which can be stolen, adapted and enhanced. Innovation should extend organisational practice beyond past experience of departments and committees.

The issues involved are discussed further in Chapter 5 on the role of the councillor and in Chapter 4 on challenging organisation assumptions as well as in the book by John Barrett and John Downs in this series on *Organising for Local Government*.

The holistic view reasserted

These themes or attributes mark out the new general management of the local authority capable of meeting the challenges and achieving the roles described in the previous chapter. The themes support each other. They must be seen as expressing and supporting the new roles of local authorities in the 1990s. Above all they must be held together by an holistic approach and a 'total' view taken.

When compared with the management of past and present, the new management – characterised as general management – captures the requirement for a holistic approach. There is a danger in such a term, however. The contemporary general management of the National Health Service has given a special and restricted meaning to the concept. In that case a new chain of command was introduced wholesale into the system replacing previous systems of administration. That is not the recipe for local government where the emergence of general management is a response to change and the inadequacies of the traditional model to meet that change. It is the blend of new approaches with the strengths of the old. Increasing recognition of the themes discussed show that general management is emerging, albeit often unrecognised. Recognition and encouragement is needed now.

Although the new challenges the adequacy of the traditional, it does not mean that the one can replace the other. A balance is required. Direct provision of services with staff employed by an authority will remain a necessary instrument of local government; the point is that it is not the only instrument; indirect provision can complement direct provision. The principles of bureaucracy help to ensure the large-scale delivery of services; yet while a bureaucratic framework may be required, responsiveness can be developed within it. Professionalism has strengths in maintaining motivation, ensuring standards and applying expertise. The issue is not the value of professional culture, but the need to create a broader culture within which professional culture can be set in perspective. The committee system ensures authoritative decision-making; the point is that its structure can be shaped differently and it need not be the only setting for the political process. The task in each case is to search for the new and to balance with the old.

General management provides countervailing forces within the organisation. Where traditional management expresses the continuity of operational management, general management expresses strategic management and policy direction. Both are required. While traditional management stresses the hierarchy of control, general management, while not denying the need for control, creates space for responsive action.

The change required should not however be seen as a once and for all change. The challenge is not the management of change or the movement from one point of stability to another, but the management of changing. This is at the heart of the new management of local government and it is general and not specific to a particular discipline. What is required is an authority capable of governing in a changing environment. The emphasis is on learning and on adapting to the learning—the core task of local government.

3 Managing for the community

Key points

▲ *An active relationship with the community is required by the enabling role and to ensure effective service for the public*

▲ *Past traditions of local admininstration have built an enclosed organisation whose barriers limit the development of both a community orientation and a public service orientation*

▲ *Management thus has to open up the authority for the enabling role and to achieve effective service for the public*

▲ *Management for the enabling role has its own requirements which are grounded in interaction and community understanding*

▲ *Effective service for the public cannot be achieved by those in the field alone; it requires public service management to set the conditions for effective service.*

A new relationship

The role of local government set out in Chapter 1 requires an active relationship between the authority and the public, both as customer and citizen. The public domain in which local government operates should provide an arena in which the public can mould the actions of public authority. Whereas in the market the public chooses from products and services made available, in the public domain the public should be able to determine the product and services available. This situation is a concept of perfect public provision; most public bodies—local authorities included—are far removed from it. Management, however, requires such a concept to determine its guiding values.

Service for the public places its own special requirements on management in local government. The day-to-day pressures mean that those requirements can easily be forgotten. Under the pressures of resource constraint, the essential rationale of public service can easily be overlooked. Yet whatever the level of resources available to local government, or whatever the activities undertaken by local authorities, their justification lies in service for the public. The local authority that seeks to carry out the role described in Chapter 1 needs a public service orientation which recognises that:

▽ its activities exist to provide service for the public
▽ it will be judged by the quality of service provided within the resources available

▽   the service provided is only of real value if it is of value to those for
    whom it is provided
▽   those for whom services are provided are customers demanding high
    quality service and citizens entitled to receive it
▽   quality of service demands closeness to the public as customer and citizen.

A local authority is not merely a provider of services, it is also a part of
government making choices on how scarce resources should be allocated
and rationing services in relation to need. It has to impose law and order, to
regulate and inspect. Those with whom it deals will not always welcome its
decisions or endorse its actions. But, as government, it acts for the public
and must act in understanding of the public, both in the decisions it makes
and in the actions it takes. The public service orientation has to be based on
that reality.

The local authority in an enabling role is not concerned merely with
the service it itself provides or the decisions it alone can make. The
enabling role involves the authority understanding the needs and problems
of the community and working with and through the community. It
requires the local authority to have an active relationship with the community
it serves as well as encouraging responsiveness on the part of those who
act on its behalf. The enabling role requires a community orientation which
recognises that the local authority:

▽   exists to serve the community of which it is itself the expression
▽   will be judged by the problems and issues it has enabled the community
    to resolve, not just by the services provided
▽   acts on behalf of the community and the citizens who constitute it
▽   must therefore be close to the community to be effective.

A close and active relationship with public as customer and citizen is
required whether in the enabling role built on an understanding of the
needs and problems of the community, and in acting with and through the
individuals and organisations that make up the community; whether in
building a public service orientation that recognises that value lies in
directly providing service *for* people; or whether acting as government
choosing, rationing and securing law and order. The local authority has
therefore to look outward to the community and to its public. It requires
both a community orientation and a public service orientation, whereas
often the past has seen an organisational orientation. Both the community
and public service orientation challenge the inward-looking enclosed
authority.

The enclosed authority

The workings of the authority have tended to focus on the production process
rather than on the marketing process. Such a focus expresses the role
of a local authority as local administration rather than as local government.
That is why the local authority has provided service *to* rather than *for* the
public or *with* or *by* the public. The authority has believed it knows what
the public needs and has not sought to learn what the public wants. For the
professional, training is believed to have given the required knowledge, but

knowledge exercised without understanding is an imperfect guide. One architect said:

> 'I have to design houses for the average tenant, and since the average tenant does not exist, I have to invent them'.

Professional authority is assumed to give the architect that right, but real tenants do exist whose views and concerns should be a measure against which professional judgement can be tested. The councillor as the elected representative has the authority to decide. He or she can too readily assume;

> 'I know what people want. I am in touch with my ward'.

As soon as one assumes one knows one ceases to learn.

Such attitudes enclose the local authority. The enclosed local authority is expressed in and reinforced by its workings :

▽ the assumption that the local authority should provide directly has meant that the local authority has not looked outward to other organisations and agencies that could be alternative providers

▽ the committee structure has focused the attention on the services provided rather than on the needs to be met and within the committee on the organisation of the service rather than on the public served

▽ the departmental structure can separate the chief officer and senior management by many tiers in the hierarchy severely limiting learning

▽ the divisions between departments can put boundaries around the concerns of a service which are not understood by the public it is designed to serve

▽ professionalism that gives a certainty of knowledge and authority action allows too little role for the public's own concerns and knowledge

▽ barriers are caused by organisational language and practice protecting the organisation but isolating it from the public served and from other organisations in the community

▽ operating procedures which derive from administrative or bureaucratic imperatives rather than the convenience, preferences or needs of the public.

All these forces help build the enclosed organisation; a number of them are further examined in the next chapter. Symptoms of the enclosed organisation are a local authority which

▽ builds its structure on the traditions of professionalism and administrative requirements rather than on the needs to be met

▽ judges the quality of service by organisational or professional standards rather than standards which reflect public demand

▽ provides no organisational space at the political or officer level to consider issues beyond those of the services currently provided or the activities of other organisations involved in the community

▽ allows no time in the working of committees to consider the quality of service provided

▽ has no means of feeding in to the working of the authority, the learning of councillors in their surgeries, of officers in the field or of other organisations in the community

▽ does not involve the public in decisions on the services provided or projects undertaken

▽ either never conducts social surveys or other forms of market research or if held has no processes for securing they are used in the working of the authority.

The impact on practice

If the barriers that support the enclosed organisation were to be broken down, the local authority would demonstrate in a myriad of ways that it was open to its community and citizens. It might, for example

▽ use new forms of public meeting in which discussion groups are formed to test out opinions

▽ institute a state of the area debate focused on the council but to which all organisations active in the community would contribute

▽ set up citizens, panels constituted to explore policy issues

▽ form an inventory of community resources, which would recognise the potential contribution of many organisations within the community

▽ develop user control of council facilities and tenant management of estates

> Middlesbrough Borough Council has set up a series of community councils. The community councils are in effect, a series of regular public meetings, which anyone from the area can attend to raise issues or to speak. They have a small budget but their main purposes include to 'extend the influence of the local community over decisions made by Middlesbrough Council and other bodies which affect the lives of the people living in those communities' and to 'encourage self-help activities that involve local people in improving the quality of life and in developing community unemployment and other initiatives'. (Middlesbrough, 1989)

▽ extend customer choice in service

> Leicester City Housing Department used a MORI poll in which it fared quite well, not to support existing practice but 'to identify our weak points — confirmation of our views in some cases but with surprises in others.
> 'The MORI Poll has allowed us to compare and contrast the attitude of people in different parts of the City, by age, social class, gender and ethnic origin. Who do we or don't we appeal to — and why ... we can now begin to home in on the markets we serve. In some cases information gaps have been identified, in others basic service delivery problems. All of these issues are now to be addressed'. (Cantle, 1989)

▽   use consultative referenda on key issues
▽   use a wide variety of modes of action beyond the direct delivery of service
▽   develop regular surveys to establish satisfaction with the services provided and processes for using the data obtained
▽   circulate households with a leaflet asking for suggestions about local authority services - making sure that all suggestions are replied to

Harlow has prepared a Citizens Charter which states:
'All citizens, irrespective of age, sex, sexuality, race, disability or income have the right
    . . . . to be heard and listened to in a respectful manner:
    . . . . of access to the authority and all those who speak on behalf of the authority;
    . . . . to clear and unambiguous information
    . . . . to fairness, equity, honesty and justice
    . . . . to be actively involved in the government of the local community
    . . . . to advocacy in upholding these rights'. (Harlow, 1989)

▽   make a public commitment that all complaints from the public be replied to within three days
▽   arrange for the design of all new buildings being discussed with those who would use them and discussed again after completion
▽   market-test new brochures, forms and notices for understanding by the public

The Chief Executive of Solihull has established a hotline which gives the public immediate access on the phone between 9.00 and 10.00 a.m. each day. 'I did it for two reasons. The first was to make some kind of statement that the organisation was approachable — a single small gesture to depreciate however marginally the often heard view that the council was remote, bureaucratic and elusive . . . The second was to help me personally to remember that despite my preoccupation with the 'macro' issues of local government administration, my job and that of my colleagues was actually all about giving satisfaction in a whole host of transactions . . .' (Scampion, 1988)

▽   develop service sampling by councillors and chief officers
▽   use quality of service for the public as a major criterion in determining rewards and promotion
▽   hold an annual quality appraisal meeting for each committee to assess the service provided, inviting public contributions
▽   supply all clients of a service with a statement of the standards of service to be aimed at and ensure that service contracts are drawn up specifying the means of redress open to them
▽   encourage senior management to spend time walking their locality, visiting, and listening to the customer

▽   arrange career movement between the local authority and other organisations serving the community.

The Wrekin District Council pioneered the use of service days as a
way of exploring the meaning of good service with the staff involved.
A service day brings together staff from all levels of the organisation to
examine a particular service. In group discussion, in pairs and in
brain-storming the service day explores what is meant by good service, what are the barriers to good service and what steps can be taken
to overcome them. The service day leads from discussion to action.
'During the day, employees, both staff and manual, are encouraged to
think constructively about the services they are responsible for providing and how they can improve the delivery of service'. (Hancox et
al, 1989)

Managing for new relationships

The organisational orientation will not easily be overcome within traditional patterns of administration. The enabling role and effective service for the
public will only be achieved if new management approaches are developed.
It has already been suggested that the effective management of the local
authority has a number of core characteristics. One can now examine the
detailed requirements of that management in two separate but inter-related
stages; firstly, the management requirements for the enabling role and then
the management requirements of effective service for the public. As will be
clear, the two are linked.

Managing for the enabling role

The enabling role requires that the council develops a management
which has:

▽   *a capacity for learning* the needs and problems faced within communities
▽   an appreciation of *community capacity* which is represented by the ability of individuals and organisations within the community to resolve
those problems
▽   an understanding of *how these capacities within the community can be
enhanced* by the local authority
▽   skills for *monitoring and review* that extend beyond the authority into
the community
▽   *new styles of leadership* by officers and members in stimulating, enlisting
and encouraging a wide range of people and interests.

A capacity for community learning

The main source of learning for the traditional local authority is
through the services provided. The administration of those services give
feedback on the demand for them, on the way they are used, and on

problems encountered. The enabling council needs a capacity for learning that extends to a wider area of concern. The enabling role, if fully developed, will require local authorities to have as wide as possible an understanding of their areas and of the problems and issues faced by their local communities, and by those who live and work within their area.

This understanding will require collecting the harder data of environmental analysis, exploring the economic, social and physical problems faced as well as gaining an understanding of the views of individuals and groups. The local authority has to develop the means of assimilating and handling this data, hard and soft. It has to be able to learn from the community in order to respond. In order to do this, the enabling council must be open to those who require its help. It cannot afford to be cut off from its public.

UNDERSTANDING COMMUNITY CAPACITY

The enabling council needs to develop an understanding of the resources that are available within the community. Beyond knowing the resources available, the council also needs an understanding of their potential for development. It is not merely what individuals and organisations can achieve now, but what they can be assisted to achieve. The council needs to understand when and how best to prompt or intervene. The understanding of the capacity to support care in the community as the Griffiths proposals are implemented makes the point well.

The local authority, moreover, stands amid a plethora of other public organisations. Central government increasingly intervenes in local community life in a wide variety of ways: by creating new organisations, giving money to existing organisations and by other forms of assistance. Local authorities can work with such organisations, utilising these resources on behalf of the community.

To judge the capacity of the community the enabling council has to build networks of understanding. It has to look constantly outward towards community resources, and through its networks of relationships to build the understanding required. These networks will already exist — in part at any rate. Elected members and officers have widespread formal and informal contacts with a whole host of organisations and individuals which can be used to help build this understanding.

ENHANCING COMMUNITY CAPACITY

The authority needs to be able to move from understanding present capacity and future potential to understanding how it can help to actually use that capacity or to realise its potential. The enabling council has to develop ways of enhancing community capacity. For example, it can:

▽   be a means of linking together organisations and individuals
▽   bring organisations or individuals together to address new concerns
▽   highlight opportunities for action from its knowledge of community needs

▽   assist through its understanding of locality
▽   use its statutory powers to assist the development of community resources
▽   provide grants or other tangible help on a one-off or continuing basis
▽   make contracts to develop or to provide goods and services
▽   regulate and control to achieve community purposes.

The council is in a position to use a wide variety of means to enhance community resources. If it is going to do this effectively it must be able to stand back and let others – organisations or individuals – take responsibility and credit. It must be able to shed its monopoly-ownership of services and share the ownership of problem-solving with others which will not be easy in a system that has depended on the opposite. In co-operating, encouraging, contracting and sharing it will be in the business of giving others confidence to do what it may once have done itself.

A CAPACITY FOR MONITORING AND REVIEW

In the enabling role the council learns and continues to learn as it enables. It is not sufficient to recognise potential or to plan to realise it. The council needs to monitor and review. It faces critical choices both as to the needs and problems to be met and the modes of working to be employed. There is a constant need to review whether the right means are being used to tackle the right ends — and to be prepared to change. The council has to recognise the need for, and the possibilities of, greater flexibility than in a traditional authority. These possibilities have constantly to be sought for; both within and beyond the council. Priorities change, and not for the council alone. Possibilities develop, and develop beyond traditional organisational boundaries. None of these can be embraced without the capacity to monitor, review and learn.

The enabling role requires that the council monitors not only its own actions but also those of others. Performance review involves the community rather than being limited to the organisation.

A NEW KIND OF LEADERSHIP

For the enabling role a new kind of leadership is required. It requires leadership which is not only capable of taking a community view but also encourages this at all levels in the organisation. Leadership needs to demonstrate that the authority is not wedded to the concerns of a particular profession or set of professions, service or set of services. Leadership itself needs to be enabling. That is to say, it needs to be helping and encouraging others both inside and outside the organisation to see issues, opportunities and needs and to respond. It is a leadership which is about empowering others to act; without a prejudice in favour of the organisation acting alone or even in control.

Such statements are easy to make and much more difficult to see translated into reality. Some of the requirements for councillors will be further discussed in Chapter 5 and those for officers in Chapter 6.

Managing for public service

The requirements of managing an effective service for the public need furthers attention. Public services are provided for the public as both customer and citizen. They are provided for the user of the service but also to achieve public purposes. A local authority is a provider of services, but it is also local government. It is public purpose which has distinguished public service provision from that which takes place solely in the private domain.

Many authorities have begun to take action to improve their relationship with the public. Reception arrangements have been made more welcoming. Social surveys have been held. Training in customer care has been developed. In short, a series of initiatives have been taken, but those initiatives only have a limited impact if they stop here and the local authority continues to be managed as if its task were just local administration. The organisational orientation will only be overcome by the explicit development of a *public service management*.

Gloucestershire County Council has developed approaches to performance management directed at achieving effective delivery of service for the public. It involves staff development interviews, departmental reviews, 3 year priority objectives, annual key tasks, departmental work programmes and committee review strategies. Underlying these approaches is a commitment to building a service culture.

The heart of effective public service management lies in meeting both user requirements and public purpose. It is a mistake to believe that public purpose necessarily eliminates all concern for the user's views on the service. Public purpose will be best fulfilled by doing as much as possible to meet user requirements. It should not be imposed by an enclosed authority, but be the expression of an active citizenship.

It is also a mistake to assume that service means that user requirements should always prevail. Resources may not be available to meet those requirements. Others needs may be greater. The local authority may protect one individual against another or pursue wider community interests. But even when user requirements cannot be met, they should be understood and explanations given of why they cannot be met. A citizen is always entitled to explanation.

At the heart of public service management is the balance between user requirements and public purpose, or between customer and citizen. Two principles should guide the balance:

▽   in shaping public purpose, the authority must be open to the public as both customer and citizen;
▽   effective service management should ensure user requirements are met within the conditions set by public purpose

It then needs to be recognised that public services differ from one another in their nature and that this has to be reflected in their management. Some of the key differences are in:

THE SERVICE ENVIRONMENT

A service may be provided in local authority premises as with a school, an old persons' home, a park or a library, but it may equally be provided in the user's premises, or wherever the user is. Social work and the home help service may take place in the home, and inspection services necessarily take place in the premises to be inspected. The fire service goes wherever fires are to be found.

There is a clear difference between services in which the local authority can manage the environment and those where the management task is to understand and work within or upon the environment. The distinction is not clear cut because the environment that is relevant to the service may not be restricted to the place where the service is provided. Understanding that environment can deepen the quality of service.

A SENSE OF TIMING

Services are provided at a particular moment of time. The extent to which the timing of the service is under the control of the local authority will vary. Fires and crimes do not wait upon the local authority, and the police and fire services are structured for immediate response. Other services can be time-tabled by appointment, while yet others control timing through other rationing processes. Each requires its own pattern of management and that pattern of management has to be appraised on the dimension of time.

THE NECESSITY OF INTERACTION

A broad distinction can be drawn between services which necessarily involve interaction between users and providers of services, such as education and social work and those in which there is no necessary interaction, such as refuse collection and street cleaning. There are other services in which there is limited interaction often to secure access to the service or as safeguards for the service, as with libraries or swimming pools. The management of the service will vary with the extent and nature of the interaction. Where the service depends on interaction there is a 'moment of truth' when staff and public service meet each other. Effective service will then depend on that 'moment of truth' (Normann, 1984).

COMPULSION AND RATIONING AS EXPRESSION OF PUBLIC PURPOSE

The public may be compelled to use a public service or as with education between 5 and 16 to show that they are obtaining the service elsewhere. Other public services involve an element of compulsion or coercion, as with the law and order services, town and country planning or inspection and regulation. The management of services will then involve the management of compulsion.

In other services the public are free to choose whether to use the service, but there the element of compulsion may be negative. Some may be denied the service because others are judged to need the service more. The management of services will then involve the management of rationing.

THE LIMITS OF PUBLIC PURPOSE

The size of the area left by public purpose for variety in response to user requirements is a critical variable, although it may depend on an authority's own decisions. The service may be designed to provide choice (as with a library service in the variety of the book stock), to impose uniform minimum standards (as with environmental health), or to respond to differing needs (as with social work). To administer for uniformity, for variety or for choice conditions the nature of service management.

THE VARIETY OF USERS

There are services in which the user can easily be identified. It is the immediate user of the service, as with a library or a sports centre, although even in those cases some would argue that wider interests are at stake. But in many public services there are many users or customers of the service. In education the child can be regarded as the customer but so can the parent, the future employer, the future spouse, all whom the child will later meet and the community at large. The management of a service directed at particular users is clearly different from that of a multi-user service, where different interests have to be balanced.

THE HEART OF SERVICE MANAGEMENT

The heart of service management is in the inter-relationships between requirements and conditions which vary from service to service and to which culture, delivery systems, organisation and management processes have to be related, and in the extent to which these support each other in the meeting of public purpose.

An authority committed to better service must think about service management — as for the new management generally — on a holistic basis, relating the various separate elements together in the whole. These will embrace its *definition* and *organisation for its provision*.

Service definition

Service definition forms the guiding principles for the management of the service. Because it expresses both public purpose and user needs it has to be formed in interaction between an authority and those who use its services.

It is a precondition of effective service management that its definition is understood by those responsible for the policies of the council, for organising the service and for providing the service, and that it can be understood by those using the service.

Service definition requires decisions on and understanding of:

▽   the reasons why the service is provided, specifying the benefits the service is designed to achieve
▽   the groups or individuals who are intended to be the direct users of the service
▽   other groups or individuals who have a concern for the service

▽   the standard to which the service should be directed in terms of what
    users can expect rather than what is to be provided
▽   the resources available for the provision of the services
▽   the priorities to be observed in the provision of the service, between
    groups, individuals and purposes
▽   the conditions which have to be observed in the provision of the ser-
    vice, expressing public purpose.

It is important that any statement of definition contains neither more
nor less detail than is required for its achievement. Space has to be left for
responsiveness in action.

Organisation for service

SERVICE CULTURE

The nature of service management is such that service can rarely be directly
controlled. It is important that management seeks to build a culture within
the organisation that supports the style of working required if the service
definition is to be realised. The culture should encapsulate public purpose
and yet reinforce the sense of service.

The service culture is not easily built if the existing culture denies
priority to it. Cultures have to be unfrozen to be built anew, but first they
have to be understood. A service culture can be expressed in statements of
values providing that they are reinforced in communication and in action.

THE ROLE OF STAFF

Many public services have their 'moment of truth' when staff and public
meet each other. In that 'moment of truth' service is made or denied.
Management cannot control this 'moment' although it determines effective
service.

Management has, however, the means to guide and structure it
through its staffing policies and practices and through definition of expec-
tation and performance, appraisal, training and development, reward systems and the like. They must all be designed to support the service
definition.

THE ROLE OF SERVICE USERS

The users of the service, and in particular the direct users, are themselves
part of the process of service provision. As such they should be seen as part
of the process of service management, guiding design, choosing alternative
forms of provision and monitoring quality. This means taking account of:

▽   the extent to which the user can and should determine the nature of the
    service received — the issue of choice
▽   the part played by the user in the process of service provision — the
    design of co-production and the role of self-help
▽   the rights of the user of the service — the issues of service standards,
    the possibility of service contracts specifying standards and rights of
    redress, enabling the user to monitor the service received

> York City Council is considering the introduction of Customer Contracts covering each of its services telling their customers:
> 'what range, standard and quality of services we intend supplying;
> how much the service costs the Council and how much it costs the customer
> what customers should do if we fail to deliver to this specification; and
> what we will do in these circumstances'. (York, 1989)

▽ learning from the user — the issue of the users' role in service design and service monitoring
▽ involving the user — the issue of user control.

THE SERVICE SETTING

The service setting is, for the user, a part of that service. Thus the management of service provision must also encompass the setting within which service happens. This includes:

▽ understanding the immediate environment
▽ learning of its role in service from those who provide and from those who use the service
▽ designing or re-designing those settings where the environment is under the control of the authority and doing whatever possible to help its use where service is provided in settings outside the authority's control.

THE ROLE OF TECHNOLOGY

Technology can aid the achievement of the service, but equally it can become a barrier to good service. It becomes a barrier if the design and use of technology is seen as an end in itself rather than a means to an end. The key issue for management must be how the technology affects other elements in the service delivery system and therefore what its effects are on the achievement of the service definition:

▽ what is the effect of technology on the environment of service?
▽ how does the technology change the role of staff and the role of users?
▽ how does the technology effect the service received by the user?

STRUCTURE

Through its organisational structure the local authority communicates as well as controls. In the design of structure for service delivery the principal guiding criterion should be the reflection of the service definition. The tests of this should be whether the structure expresses the service definition and supports effective service management.
    Some of the issues that have to be faced are:

▽ the number of tiers in the hierarchy as these can be barriers to effective communication for service management
▽ the grouping of activities as these may not relate to the service provided as defined by the service definition
▽ barriers within the organisation which may prevent the ready assembly of skills, information and staff to meet service needs
▽ the role of the centre which can limit the capacity to provide effective service by controlling rather than supporting and helping.

MANAGEMENT PROCESSES

The management processes of an organisation must both guide the provision of services and learn from the experience. They must express both the requirements of public purpose and the needs of the service user. The management processes of the authority must ensure:

▽ the setting of requirements for service provision, so that those involved understand the nature of public purpose
▽ the setting of parameters for service provision, so that managers understand the resources available, the conditions for their use and their scope for responsiveness in action
▽ the establishment of processes for reviewing achievement and developing the organisation to overcome problems
▽ learning processes to guide management in the development of the service definition
▽ processes which devolve management responsibility as near to the point of service delivery as possible.

SERVICE LEADERSHIP

If public purpose and the service definition are the driving force of service provision and its management there will be a need for leadership devoted to this at all levels in the organisation but particularly at senior management level. The ability to inspire and motivate staff, to innovate and develop service and to be their own agents for change, as well as to understand and marry the needs and interests of service users with those of the organisation and its personnel are essential. This will involve:

▽ setting standards and promoting quality both for *what* is to be done and *how* it is done
▽ evaluating people and judging levels of motivation, energy and capacity with consequent attention to praise, encouragement, constructive criticism and learning
▽ defining and promoting role models within the organisation which will influence others as well as setting personal standards which can be clearly seen
▽ challenging and re-framing the conventions which underlie the service and the way it operates at the same time as identifying and maintaining the 'basics'
▽ encouraging and, above all, communicating (listening as well as telling).

The holistic view again

Both in developing management for the enabling role and in developing service management a holistic approach is required. The elements that make up effective management have to be considered not in isolation but in their inter-relationship to each other. Thus effective service direction will not develop through management processes alone. It requires service leadership and service culture, but if these are denied in the procedures of the authority service management will be seen as mere rhetoric that has no meaning in practice. Equally, policies to enhance community capacity, which are not based on learning from the community, will be unrealistic just as learning that is developed beyond the capacity to use it leads only to frustration.

For management of the enabling role and for public service management as for the new general management of which they are particular expressions, a total view is needed. Without it the management of the authority will be unbalanced. It is in achieving balance in the development of the elements that effective management is achieved.

Postscript: consumerism is not enough

Much recent debate has emphasised consumerism. Consumerism has much to contribute to local government, if by that is meant a concern for the individual customer. Consumerism, while valuable, is, however, not by itself enough to open up the local authority. For a local authority is more than an organisation providing services to the individual customer:

▽   in the enabling role the local authority looks outward to the community
▽   in the community the public is both customer and citizen
▽   in public services both public purpose and customer requirements have to be met
▽   in public service there may be many customers, for many can benefit from the service beyond the immediate user.

What is required is not mere consumerism, but the community focus of the enabling role and a public service orientation that recognises both customer and citizen. These should guide the development of management in opening up the enclosed authority to the drive of a wider imperative.

4   Challenging the old to build new organisational structures

Key points

▲ *The organisation of the local authority is conditioned by the necessities of what has been required in the past and the assumptions which have been built around them*

▲ *These assumptions have to be challenged if local authorities are to adjust to a new role*

▲ *The assumptions support the traditional patterns of working in departments, within professional boundaries and structured around hierarchies of control (and, as later discussed, of committees)*

▲ *Once the assumptions have been challenged new forms of organisation can be developed to support the new role*

The pervasiveness of organisational assumptions

The pervasiveness of received assumptions has already been explored. In every organisation there is a set of assumptions about the way that the organisation should be structured and should carry out its work. These assumptions are rarely stated because they are so much a part of the organisation that they do not need to be. They are grounded in past experience and reinforced in the present. They determine future experience because they limit the consideration of organisational possibilities to those that lie within their boundaries and grasp. Possibilities that lie beyond them will probably not even be considered. Such assumptions build continuity into the working of the organisation. The problem only comes when change is more important than continuity.

Organisational assumptions are necessarily based on past roles and known tasks and conditions. They are, therefore, likely to reflect behaviour appropriate to those roles, tasks and conditions. So long as these remain more or less unchanged the organisational assumptions can guide behaviour, but if they change significantly it may be necessary to reconsider the assumptions. Such a period has been reached in local government with the massive changes forcing the new role of local authorities which has already been outlined.

Existing structures and processes reflect the old role of local authorities. A set of organisational assumptions grounded in and supporting the role of the local authority as the local administration of service provision underpins them. As the role of the local authority as local government develops, then those organisational assumptions will be challenged and new ideas emerge.

That is easier said than done. The assumptions are so much a part of the working of the organisation that they are taken for granted. The challenge is to think beyond the confines of past assumptions. The first stage in this is to make the assumptions explicit. Only then is it possible to generate new thinking by opening up different possibilities appropriate to new conditions and changed circumstances.

The constraining assumptions explored

This chapter will explore the re-thinking necessary to develop the kind of organisation to sustain the role of the local authority as local government. In doing so it will clarify the key assumptions which reinforce present patterns of working and which restrict development. In particular the assumptions that:

▽   a local authority shall itself provide directly all the services for which it is responsible and so should employ all the staff and own the main resources necessary for the provision of those services — the assumption of self-sufficiency

▽   a local authority should normally provide a standard uniform service on a universal basis — the assumption of uniformity

▽   councillors, by the fact of election, are able to speak and act on behalf of those they represent on all the issues before the council — the representative principle

▽   the professional officers have the authority and the knowledge to make the necessary judgements on what is needed in the service provided — the professional principle

▽   in order to exercise effective control councillors and officers have to control events *as they happen* through direct hierarchical control — the principle of direct control

▽   the local authority is constituted to provide services on a continuing basis — the principle of continuity.

These assumptions are reflected in characteristic modes of working which support and express them. In particular, the main work of the officers is conducted through a series of service and central departments constituted on a professional basis and organised according to principles of hierarchy and uniformity — the departmental mode of operation. In parallel, as will be shown in the next chapter, the main work of councillors is conducted through committees with their own characteristic mode of working.

The assumption of self-sufficiency

For a long time it has been assumed that if local authorities have been given responsibility for a service, they should provide that service directly through their own organisation and should themselves employ all the staff and own all the resources required for the provision of services.

The assumption can be found in common-place remarks such as:

'We cannot use voluntary bodies to provide main-line services because a local authority has to maintain standards.'

'Joint action between local authorities will rarely work. Each local authority has to be in charge of its own service.'

'A local authority has to be large enough to ensure it can provide the specialist services it requires.'

The assumption has meant not merely that local authorities have rarely considered contracting out their services or the wide-scale use of voluntary provision, but that even joint action between authorities has seldom been seen as a practical option. Indeed, so deep has been the assumption that alternative means of providing services have not even been discussed. They have simply not been considered. Direct provision has been seen as the only way of doing things.

It has meant, too, that in the long and unproductive debates about local government re-organisation, the size of local authorities has been assumed to be governed by the necessities of direct provision rather than by perceptions of local community. It has even been argued that the size of local authorities should be governed by their capacity to employ specialist staff or deploy specialist services. The sharing of staff between authorities, the use of part-time staff, or the use of external specialist services has not been given serious consideration.

Yet there is no necessary reason why self-sufficiency should be assumed. The enabling role challenges the assumption by suggesting the wide variety of ways in which a local authority can act. The enabling council has neither to assume the necessity of direct provision nor deny its possibility. It focuses attention on the most effective way of meeting needs and problems. How the authority secures the staff or other resources it requires becomes an issue for discussion rather than one hidden beneath the concept of self-sufficiency.

Once it becomes not just acceptable but necessary to ask how a service can best be provided and by whom, the organisation is looked at in a different way. With work being undertaken in new ways, more flexible styles and structures become necessary. The organisation must be structured to assist rather than to inhibit managing and working across organisational boundaries.

The assumption of uniformity

The local authority is structured to provide universal services on a uniform basis. Universality and uniformity have again been assumed to be a necessary part of local government. This assumption derives in part from the role of local authorities as monopoly or near monopoly providers. It has meant that:

▽   public provision has limited choice, because universality sees no need for choice and uniformity sees no case for the diversity from which choice can be made

▽ local authorities have rarely studied the distribution of their resources
between different areas, groups or individuals, because uniform services universally available have been thought to allow no possibility of
discrimination — equity has been assumed to be automatic rather than
something that has to be worked for
▽ the new local authorities after the 1970s re-organisation strove to
introduce common policies throughout their area, even though
their predecessor authorities had pursued different policies; uniformity was seen as necessary for a new authority so the reasons for
the differences were not even explored; uniformity then quickly
became valued in itself. Services are often controlled according to
standard rules to ensure uniformity of practice, even where needs
vary.

Underlying the assumption has been a presumption of common and
shared needs. Even in fields, such as social services, that are not structured
for universal provision, the emphasis has been on uniform provision. It has
meant that for most of local government there has been too little exploration either of the diversity of need or the possibility of diversity of provision. Uniformity has been its own justification. It is difference that has had
to be justified. This has, of course, reinforced the idea of local authorities
being universal providers since only in this way is it believed possible to
ensure uniformity.

The enabling role challenges both universality and uniformity. Once it
is accepted that in an enabling authority a service can be provided in a
variety of ways, then it follows that there can be more than one provider.
Equally, if the council is concerned to enable the community to meet the
needs, opportunities and problems faced, then there is a requirement to
recognise diversity where needs, opportunities and problems vary.

Once the assumption of uniformity, supported by universality is challenged it opens up the need for the authority to learn more about the differing needs and problems it faces and of the differential impact of its activities
on different groups. It helps the local authority to appreciate that uniformity of practice can discriminate against those with different needs. It opens
up, too, the possibility that a local authority may see a diversity of providers
and a diversity of practice as a positive asset.

Challenging the assumptions of universality and uniformity puts on to
the agenda of political and management concern such issues as:

▽ the analysis of the differential impact of local authority activities
▽ the extent of and possibilities for choice in public provision

Cheshire County Council has carried out a study of the use of county
services, which amongst other aspects examined 'whether the use of
particular services and county council services in general are distributed more towards particular types of household. It analyses how
that use of services is distributed between different groups of households, distinguishing them by tenure, household income and social/
economic group. It is designed to assist policy-makers in planning
future provision.' (Cheshire 1989)

▽ the management of rationing or of matching resources to different needs
▽ the management of a multiple set of providers
▽ closer targeting of resources to identified needs
▽ encouragement of variety in professional and management practice
▽ the real distribution of resources.

The organisation required to manage diversity will be very different from the organisation required to enforce uniformity. The emphasis of the former will be on creating space for responsiveness in action, while the emphasis of the latter will be on detailed control.

The representative principle

Local authorities are elected authorities. The councillor and the council are elected as representatives of the community. It is from the fact of election that they gain their authority and it is that fact that gives them legitimacy in acting on behalf of those they represent. None of this can be contested. Indeed it will be argued in Chapter 5 that the representative role receives inadequate support. What can be contested is whether the representative principle, necessary though it is, is sufficient. It is too readily assumed that because the council consists of elected representatives, that is a sufficient expression of local democracy. Although the councillors can be said to be elected to speak on behalf of the people, it does not necessarily follow that they know what the people want them to say.

The issue is not the representative principle as an expression of local democracy, but its monopoly. The belief that the representative principle is a sufficient expression of people's wishes can lead to a neglect of other means of expression. Both councillors and officers can easily come to say and to think:

'Councillors are elected to make decisions — if people don't like it they can get rid of them at the next election.'
'The councillor represents all the people, unlike pressure groups which only represent a section of the people.'
'Councillors do not need market research to tell them what people think: they have surgeries and meet people on the doorstep and in the clubs all the time.'

The danger is that insistence of the sufficiency on the representative principle weakens rather than strengthens local democracy. It can mean a failure by officers and members to develop other means of learning from the public, because the councillor is assumed to know, or worse still, not to need to know the public view. It can mean resistance to the development of direct user involvement in the way services are organised (for example, in the management of estates or in the control of leisure centres) as if in some strange way this would undermine the position of the council. Such a view rests upon an impoverished concept of local government. If the role of the local authority is to enable the community to meet its needs and problems in the most effective way, it requires a local authority capable of learning and acting in many ways, including assisting individuals and groups to resolve issues directly. However sensitive or sophisticated the elected councillor, he or she will not be enough. The elected council will play a key role but will need to be supported through the different kinds of approaches suggested in Chapter 3 and take account of the considerations set out in Chapter 5.

The professional principle

If the political structure is dominated by the representative principle, then the officer structure is dominated by the professional principle. It is assumed that the management of the local authority's work should be conducted through departments which match areas of service and in which the dominant positions are defined and held by a particular profession. Professionalism as an organisational principle defines the boundaries between departments and the working within them.

Professionalism brings great strengths. The local authority needs to be able to call upon and to use professional skills in a variety of ways. What is at stake is not the need for professionalism and for professionals, but the use of professionalism as an organising principle of local authorities. In Chapter 6 its role as the basis for staff development in local government will be discussed. The effect of professionalism can be to introduce rigidity into the working of the local authority by reinforcing boundaries, maintaining existing practice and creating barriers to learning. In its turn organisational continuity can reinforce rigidity in professionalism. Organisational and professional continuities reinforce each other.

The wider the interests of the local authority, and as local government these will be those of the whole community, the more likely it is going to be that issues will cut across and so make nonsense of the boundaries between professions. The traditional match between professions and areas of service provision has served local government well but is no longer enough.

It becomes destructive, however, when it gets in the way of handling the issues facing the authority. The constraints imposed by professional dominance have to be loosened. In dealing with the environmental issues and the political challenge of the 'Green' lobby, many authorities have not re-framed the issue but seen it in terms of conventional professional interests as environmental health and planning.

The dominance of the professional principle in the working of the local authority is so readily assumed that alternative patterns of organisation are rarely considered. But an emphasis on local government challenges that principle. It places the emphasis on understanding the community's perception of their needs and problems rather than relying on the professional definition of those needs and problems. It also opens up the possibility of different modes of working which may not necessarily require the direct employment of professionals and thus paves the way to possible new forms of organisation. It could mean:

▽   new bases for the division of the work of the authority related to geography, to issues, to clients or to mode of working
▽   an emphasis on collective organisational values — reflecting the enabling role — which rise above professional values
▽   changing and developing career patterns unfettered by professional practice

▽ intelligence and information services unconstrained by professional
    boundaries.

The principle of direct control

Any organisation needs to control the activities for which it is responsible
whether those activities are undertaken directly or indirectly. In the workings of the local authority it has been assumed, however, that control has to
be exercised directly and immediately. Local authorities are structured to
exercise control 'as it happens', even though such control can never be fully
possible. Yet so deep is the assumption of direct control that its ineffective-
ness and impracticality is rarely exposed.

The committees of local authority control, in theory if not in practice,
the services for which they are responsible. The committee is assumed to
exercise control through a hierarchy of command expressed in the multi-
tiered organisations which are the departments of local authorities. The
length of the hierarchy gives expression to the search for direct control in
detail.

The search for direct control is a search that is self-defeating. The scale
and complexities of most local authority activities can never be controlled
directly. However, the attempt to do so has:

▽ focused the attention of councillors on the working of the organisation
    rather than on what is required from the organisation
▽ restricted the capacity of managers to deploy effectively their resources
    in relation to the tasks to be undertaken
▽ reduced, through the constraining influence of the hierarchy, the
    capacity for innovation and responsiveness
▽ limited, in the length of its hierarchies, the capacity for organisation to
    act quickly or often even decisively.

The enabling role challenges the assumption of direct control. Where
the local authority acts through other organisations it cannot control directly; if it wishes to control it will be through indirect means by contracts or
agreements. In competitive tendering the local authority has already moved
from control 'as it happens' to control through specification and monitoring. Instead of the self-defeating attempt to control on a continuing basis, a
new rhythm of control is established based on:

▽ pausing to specify what is required
▽ letting go to allow freedom in action
▽ pausing to monitor and review.

Rather than control directly, control is exercised through planning and
review. Even indirect control may be inappropriate for the enabling role. If
the local authority is genuinely working with its community to identify and
meet needs and opportunities, it will sometimes play little or no part in
subsequent action once this has been stimulated. From direct control it will
have moved to influence and encouragement. Its concern will be how to
exercise influence and how to position itself to encourage. Work will not be
formally contracted or agreed and what is being done will be on behalf of
the community at large and not specifically the council.

The organisational structures of local authorities express in their multi-tiered hierarchies the principle of direct control. New structures must assist the development of indirect control and the management of influence.

The principle of continuity

Any organisation is to a degree structured for continuity. The very word *organisation* presupposes a certain continuity and structure imposes its own rigidity. The necessity of continuity becomes a danger if it becomes so much a part of the working organisation that it excludes consideration of the need for, or perception of, the possibility of change.

Because local authorities have come to see themselves as agencies for the delivery of an established pattern of services, the assumptions of continuity have become an organisational necessity expressed in a wide variety of ways:

▽   the dominance of the professional model with its emphasis on an established body of knowledge learnt at the start of the career and defined in its application through the career

▽   career paths following tracks laid by past experience, reinforcing that experience

▽   barriers built by discrimination and inertia which mean that the organisation reproduces itself in recruitment, in training and in promotion

▽   hierarchies of control reinforcing established practice and limiting the learning of future possibilities

▽   committees focusing on organisation continuity rather than on organisational change.

The enabling role challenges the assumption of organisational continuity because it challenges the role of the local authority as being about only the direct provision of an established series of service. The role of local authorities as local government requires a capacity to learn and respond to the needs and problems of the local community. By opening up the possibility of many different modes of action, the enabling role challenges the continuities of existing practice expressed in the organisation of direct service provision.

A totally changing organisation is not required. This would be neither practicable nor desirable. What is required is an organisation with the capacity to change built into its working alongside the continuities necessary to any organisation. Change and continuity have to be balanced in the working of the authority.

This means that managers have continually to read their organisation in its working not so that continuity is removed, but so that countervailing forces can be incorporated to open up the possibility of change. This may mean that a capacity for learning and for adaptation needs to be built into organisational structures, so overcoming the constraints which hierarchy and other inhibiters place on organisational change.

Reconsideration of the organisational building blocks

The interplay of these assumptions has created two organisational building blocks which condition the way the authority works:

▽ the committees as the main setting for the playing out of the councillor role, and
▽ the department as the organisation and focus for the officer structure.

Both committee and department have been formed by the organisation, yet they are so central to it that it is difficult to think of them apart from the organisation and difficult to think of the organisation of the local authority without committee and department structures in their traditional forms.

Just as new roles challenge the organisational assumptions inherited from the past, so they also challenge the meaning given by past practice to committees and to departments and prompt the need to consider alternative meanings and structures. The next chapter will review the committee system in its impact on the councillor; this chapter focuses on the department.

By convention local authorities have been structured into a series of departments. That is hardly surprising. Any organisation beyond a minimum size has to divide up its work in order to carry out its tasks. What is perhaps surprising is the remarkable degree of uniformity both in the overall departmental system and in the structure within departments.

In local government's case the department means:

▽ responsibility for a service of the authority or for one of its central functions
▽ issues which cross boundaries between departments being forced into an existing structure or, possibly, being contained within a specially created department
▽ the boundaries of the services or the central functions being defined by the professions
▽ the dominance within the department of a profession and its culture
▽ a multi-tiered hierarchy of control
▽ a focus on direct provision of the services
▽ central departments exercising detailed control over the use of resources
▽ direct employment of all staff required and deployment of the resources needed for the provision of the services
▽ a bureaucratic mode of working based on the principles of hierarchy and uniformity.

These structures reflect the organisational assumptions we have discussed. Once those assumptions are challenged new possibilities can be realised. Some of the approaches that can be or are being developed are set out below, each of them challenging the traditional model of the department.

New bases for structural division

It is possible to conceive of the work of the authority being divided up in different ways. A recent study by the Norwegian Association of Local Authorities has explored the possibility of alternatives to departments based on the main functions (for example education, social services, planning, etc). It has proposed two possibilities. The first is division of the work into geographical areas. The second is division of work according to the type of activity: regulatory, service provision, and developmental, because each requires a different type of organisation. The research argues that regulatory activities require a bureaucratic mode, service provision requires a decentralised mode, while developmental activities require an organic mode. The Association's work also explored the possibility of basing the structure on the type of client, old people; children etc, but found it impracticable. The study has challenged past assumptions just as they are being challenged here by events. In our system most interest has been shown in developing structures which are based on geographical units though there has also been interest in creating organic, developmental working.

> Tower Hamlets has organised its activities through seven neighbourhood committees composed of the elected councillors for the area, with neighbourhood chief executives and other chief officers. These committees have their own budgets and are responsible for much of the work of the council. They are matched by neighbourhood organisations for service delivery.

What is important is not one particular approach but that there exist other ways than those assumed to be inevitable. Some of the changes taking place and some of the further possibilities are listed below.

The client-contractor split

The legislation on compulsory competitive tendering has made local authorities divide the client function (of specifying what is required and ensuring its delivery) from the contractor role of providing the service. It has led to the creation of Direct Service Organisation separated from the departments in which they have traditionally been placed. This development has led some local authorities, particularly district councils, to carry out radical reviews of their whole organisation to incorporate an overall distinction between client and contractor roles.

A challenge to the dominance of professionalism

To reduce the danger of narrow professionalism some local authorities have re-grouped departments to bring together within a directorate different professional groups (for example, Directorates of Community Services or Directorates of Technical Services). Such changes may be important symbolically but probably do not effect the dominance of professionalism. The building blocks within directorates seem to remain unchanged and suggest that narrow professionalism will probably be more effectively contained by the development of general management.

Cross-cutting structures

As already argued an organisation has to divide up its work in order to carry out its business. Dangers arise when the divisions restrict the capacity of the organisation to deal with problems and issues which do not fit easily into that structure. They will become more serious in a rapidly changing environment, since present structures are built for past problems. Local authorities need a capacity to look across departments to identify those things not being properly handled—a strategic centre. They also require a capacity to work across departments, using such devices as area teams, project teams, programme teams, policy groups, and so on.

The devolution of management responsibility

Once it is accepted that control does not have to be exercised directly, but can be exercised through setting targets to be met within given resources, then the basis has been laid for devolved responsibility to managers, who can then be held responsible for the targets. Devolved management responsibility opens up the possibility of new forms of organisation and of new relationships between, say, service departments and other departments. Devolution of responsibility nearer to the point of service delivery is likely to mean greater responsiveness to service users.

A reduction of hierarchy

There are departments in which at least eight tiers constitute the hierarchy of command. As the need for learning is recognised, each tier comes to be seen as a barrier to learning from the experience of those who face issues in the field. As the strategic role of the organisation's centre is recognised, each tier comes to be seen as a barrier to the identification and communication of purpose. Devolved management will replace detailed central control rendering unnecessary the hierarchies that re-enforced it.

Wansdyke District Council has abandoned the traditional departmental structure and has appointed a district general manager who is responsible to the council for the performance of the authority. Direct service managers are responsible to the District Managers for achieving the required level of performance. One service manager is reported as saying 'I have much more freedom to control my own destiny. I report now direct to the district general manager. He sets the targets and I'm free to achieve them in the way I think best and I can choose my own staff'. (Murray 1989)

Central control and support services

The central departments have traditionally been dominated not by the strategic role, but by their role in controlling departments and in the provision of support services. A control function will remain, even as management is devolved, but the function is changed from control over detail to control for overall results. It is for the manager responsible to determine how those results are to be achieved. For this reason it is for departments themselves to determine what support services they require and to determine whether they should provide them themselves or obtain them from a central department or elsewhere. In this environment central departments will probably put their services on a trading basis and so create entirely new forms of relationship and culture. (These issues are examined from the point of view of the Treasurer's Department in the book by David Rawlinson and Brian Tanner on *Financial Management in the 1990s* in this series).

> Lincolnshire County Council is introducing service level agreements to govern the business relationship between internal clients and internal contractors. They will be brief and non-technical in legal terms. They will however specify service quality, quantity and price. There will be, for example 'separated contractor organisations covering legal, financial and property and personal services. These organisations would cover such services and activities in both central and service departments so that they are all carried out in a separated client/contractor role'. This is part of a review designed to change the organisation and structure 'to secure maximum economy, efficiency and effectiveness in a new environment'. (Lincolnshire 1989)

The strategic centre

If local authorities are really to be local government, they need to develop to the full the capacity to support the role. That requires from the local authority a capacity to identify community needs, set strategies and ensure the organisational or inter-organisational capacity to achieve that strategy. The role of the council requires support from the organisation. This requirement gives meaning to the role of the chief executive and creates a need for a strategic centre to the organisation which can oversee those processes and tasks.

Working with and through other organisations

If it is accepted that local authorities as local government can play an enabling role working with and through other organisations, then their approach to organisation is fundamentally changed. Organisation no longer means an organisation under direct control. It may be an organisation with which the authority has drawn up a contract. It may be one to which it has given a grant. It may be one the authority has pressed for action. Organisational management becomes inter-organisational management.

New organisation creation

In inter-organisational management, the local authority can itself build

> Rochford District Council has promoted what is in effect a management buy-out based on a leisure management company, CIRCA Leisure Services to take over the work of its leisure department, employing most of its staff, but on new conditions. (Cooke 1989)

new forms of organisation. It can encourage tenant co-operatives. It can allow management buy-outs subject to safeguards. It can form companies or create trusts. Partnerships can be formed with the private sector.

Northamptonshire County Council have reviewed the structure of central services, following a consultants report which identified the need for effective arrangements 'to provide advice for the strategic management of the county council in responding to the challenges of the 1990s'. The council has decided to constitute a corporate head-quarter under the chief executive with the Director of Finance and Administration, the Director of Personnel and an Assistant Chief Executive for 'Policy planning and review, public relations, research and information and emergency planning'. At the same time a Director of Professional Services has been appointed to be responsi-ble for the management of support services on a commercial basis, including legal services, accountancy services etc. The structure sup-ports the role of the chief executive in strategic management. (Northamptonshire)

These changes and possibilities show how alternatives to the organisa-tion of local authorities based on departments in their traditional form can be developed once the assumptions that constrain thinking are challenged. Those assumptions are grounded in past roles and past ways of working. The new role of local authorities as local government and the development of general management lead to the challenge to organisational assump-tions. New patterns of organisation are required. The department as it has been known need no longer be taken as the key building block; professional boundaries need not be so rigid; and hierarchies of control need no longer dominate. It is necessary to took beyond these things if local authorities are to sustain their role as local governement. But that is not enough. Equally changes are required in the organisation built to support or to confine the councillor's roles.

5   Developing the councillors role for local government

Key points

▲ *The general management of local government needs to be set in a political environment which enhances the changed role of the local authority*

▲ *The organisation of the local authority has not supported the full range of councillor roles*

▲ *In effect, the committee system has focused the councillor's attention on the day to day working of departments*

▲ *The policy and management roles now required are different and challenge the workings of the traditional committee system which provide too little organisational time and space for learning, direction and review*

▲ *The representative role of the councillor gains a new importance in the enabling council, but needs to be supported in the working of the authority.*

Roles and responsibilities

As the role of the council and its management change so must the role of the councillor. The re-shaping taking place makes the role of the councillor more not less important, but that role will not, and cannot, be played in the way it has previously been played. New processes and new settings will be required to support it. An analysis of the present roles and responsibilities of councillors and of the processes and settings by which the council supports those roles is necessary. Those processes and settings have often not given adequate support to the full range of roles. The recent changes in local government have led to a questioning of past processes and settings and to innovation and experiment. Futher innovation and development is now required.

The councillor has many responsibilities which create different roles:

▽ responsibility as an elected representative for an area with a concern for the interests of the area and for those who live within it

▽ responsibility as an elected representative for the authority as a whole and the communities it represents

▽ responsibility as a member of the council for the policies of the authority

▽   responsibility as a member of the council for the effective working of the organisation.

One can distinguish between the representative role expressing the first two responsibilities, and the policy and management roles. The effective council should recognise and support all these roles since they are necessarily linked. The policy and management roles are justified by the representative roles and the representative roles are given expression in the other roles. In practice councils too often have given little support to the representative roles only giving real support to the policy and management ones.

Traditional patterns of working

As already suggested, unquestioned assumptions mean that the councillor's life has been dominated by the operation of the committee system. The committee system has focused on the services provided by the authority; it has identified councillors with particular committees and their services rather than with the business of the council as a whole. Within committees, the agenda has concentrated the attention of councillors on the detailed organisation and running of those services. The attention of councillors has been concentrated less on their role as representatives of the local community deciding what should be provided than on the on-going process of deciding how it should be provided. This concern has so absorbed the work of committees that there has often been little attention paid to reviewing what has actually been achieved. Performance review, if it has been carried out, often has not been part of the basic work of the service committee, but has been isolated as a function of a separate performance review committee.

The regular cycle of meetings has reinforced the routinisation of the work of committees. Agendas fill up with items that have to be decided immediately, focusing attention on the day-to-day running of the department; if a major item of policy has to be dealt with, it will be merely another item on an already overloaded agenda. Sense of direction or purpose is lost in the detail. The undifferentiated cycle in which all meetings have the same type of agenda and are conducted in the same way according to the formalities of committee business, allows insufficient organisational time or space for councillors to set directions for the services for which they are responsible, to explore in depth new policy issues or to review effectively the workings of the service and department.

The traditional committee system has apparently supported the councillors responsibility for the working of the organisation. It has, perhaps, too readily been assumed that responsibility for the working of the organisation is most effectively exercised through what has been described as 'control as it happens' involving committees in detailed operational decisions.

While there will always be detailed decisions that require political judgement because for example, they are potentially contentious in the public arena, the mistake is to assume that responsibility for the working of the organisation has to or even can be exercised directly. The attempt to do so may only lead to frustration, as councillors lose direction in the search for detailed control.

The pressures for change

The need for change in the way councils work has increasingly been recognised by many local authorities. The research carried out for the 1986 *Report of the Widdicombe Inquiry* into the conduct of local authority business contained descriptions of the way in which the role of the councillor, and relationships between councillors and officers, had been and were continuing to change (Widdicombe 1986). This had been caused by:

▽ changing politics
▽ the emergence of more assertive politics
▽ the weakening of consensus
▽ the questioning of past professional solutions to many of local government's problems
▽ frustration with often apparently slow-moving and unresponsive bureaucratic organisations
▽ the desire to make sure that new policies were actually being implemented.

From left, right and centre has come a push for a new view of the councillor's role. Many of the assumptions and conventions which had governed the past are being called into question and new approaches are being developed and tested.

Local authorities have begun to develop new ways of working. These have involved:

▽ review of the structure and remit of committees
▽ developing the role of the policy and resources committee
▽ the development of working parties and panels (often bringing together officers and members) for policy development monitoring and review
▽ the creation of area committees to give recognition to the councillor's representative role and to geography as well as function
▽ the use of seminars and away days and so on

Notwithstanding this, however, in nearly every authority the committee remains the focus of the councillor's work. For all that is said about change and diversity in local government, it is the permanence and the uniformity of the committee system that is striking.

A new and clear challenge to past ways of working comes from the advent of compulsory competitive tendering; not least because it has forced attention to be given to the desired standard of service and how it should be defined. Obvious as this issue sounds, there has traditionally been little explicit consideration of standards of provision and, thus, of whether they are being met. Where a service is contracted out (or contracted in) time and consideration have to be given by councillors to laying down what is required of a service, so that detailed specifications can be drawn up. Councillors can no longer control 'as it happens'. What is specified beforehand is all that will be delivered, unless the council wishes to undertake the difficult and expensive process of negotiating a variation to the contract. Once the contract is drawn up, the emphasis is on monitoring and review to ensure the service is delivered as required. Specification, monitoring and review apply whether the service is contracted out or contracted within the orgainsation.

In the case of internal contracting another issue is raised. The role of councillors in relation to the internal Direct Service Organisation (DSO) cannot be the one to which they have become accustomed in service committees. A DSO tied to the traditional pattern of committee working would soon be ineffective and incapable of taking decisions with the speed required to provide a competitive service. Moreover, councillors cannot behave in the same way and at the same time as client and contractor. Consequently, some local authorities are making their DSOs responsible to a management board. This will operate with different ground rules to the conventional committee; it may include officers as well as councillors; and it will be capable of quick decision making. These developments show that councillors need not control 'as it happens' but can achieve effective control by specifying what is required and ensuring it is achieved. This development alone challenges the past patterns of committee working.

Such patterns have to be changed if local authorities are to respond to the trends set out in Chapter 1. The focus of committees on the on-going processes of departmental working may be appropriate if the task of local authorities is seen as local administration but not if they are seen as local government capable of responding to the challenges faced.

A check-list of current issues

In summary, the events and changes in local government over the last few years have highlighted a series of issues about the roles of councillors and the way these are given expression in the workings of local authorities. It is not so much that these are new issues but rather that too often they have not been properly addressed. They now *have* to be addressed. They are summarised in the following questions:

▽ Is there an understanding of the different roles of the councillors?
▽ Is there adequate support for those roles?
▽ Are all the councillors expected to fulfil all roles in equal measure or should there be a differentiation of roles?
▽ Are there adequate processes and procedures for the councillors setting direction for the authority and for its services, making policy and allocating resources, providing for political priorities and requirements?
▽ How are councillors' responsibilities for the organisation and for the effectiveness of operational management best discharged and are they better discharged through setting direction and review of performance than by detailed control?
▽ Are there adequate processes and procedures for monitoring and review of the achievement both of policy and performance?
▽ What settings exist for the development of policy? Do they permit the full involvement of councillors and officers in that development?
▽ Is there a process of committee review in which their working is regularly appraised by councillors? Does the structure of committees fit what the authority is trying to do? Does the working of committees, their agendas and procedures enable councillors to discharge their organisational responsibilities?

▽   What are the implications of compulsory competitive tendering for the role of the member and the structure of committees?

▽   How does the authority handle issues which fall within the remit of more than one committee? How does it handle issues which are not at present within the remit of any committees? How does it identify such issues?

▽   Are new settings needed to develop effective working partnerships between the political and officer structures?

▽   Is the representative role of the councillors adequately recognised in organisation of the authority? Does the organisation of the council assist them to discharge their responsibilities?

▽   Are there adequate support services for councillors?

Supporting the policy and management role

These foregoing questions relate both to the councillors' representative roles and to their policy and management roles. Policy and management roles are given expression in the committee system but, as already shown, this gives inadequate support to these roles and is likely to prove increasingly inadequate. Chapter 2 has shown that the management processes which are necessary need to be governed by political processes if local authorities are to be truly local government. The councillor clearly has a key role in the general management of the authority.

If management is to be subjected to effective political control, there must be special emphasis on the role of the councillor in the learning processes of the authority, in setting strategy and policy direction and in reviewing performance. It is never possible to separate the roles of councillors and officers in absolute terms. Councillors have a responsibility for all that happens in a local authority even though they do not exercise that responsibility directly. Where they do exercise responsibilities directly, as they should in strategy and policy direction, they should draw upon officer advice and guidance. Analysis has suggested that the existing patterns of the committee system neglect such things as learning, strategy, direction and review in favour of control as it happens. CCT has already shown that there are other ways of working and this points clearly to the issue of what changes are required to enable the roles of the councillor in policy-making and management to be given the support required on the broader front.

This requires a different approach which focuses the councillors attention on:

▽   changes in the environment and needs in the community

▽   setting direction, specifying policy and the requirements for the organisation

▽   devolving responsibility for meeting those requirements

▽   reviewing achievement and organisational effectiveness.

Regular re-appraisal

The committee system both in its structure and its way of working should be seen as an instrument to enable the councillors to play their policy and management roles. As an instrument it can be effective or ineffective and if ineffective it should be changed. Too often it is assumed that the committee system has to be accepted as a basic part of local government. It is, with certain exceptions, for each council to determine the settings in which business is done and the way it is done. The committees system should be subject to regular review by those whose instrument it is, that is the councillors.

Local authorities should hold periodic surveys of councillors' views on the committee system, on the use of working parties and seminars, and on the support they get. If service for the customer is important to the authority, then the councillor is the customer of administrative services. A survey is the starting point for review. One test in any review should be to question what issues and what operations the committee system focuses on and what issues and what operations are being neglected.

A committee system expresses in its structure a viewpoint on the role of the local authority, the tasks it carries out and its way of working. The danger is that the structure freezes the viewpoint, so that past roles and tasks determine both present and future performance. The process of review goes beyond structure to the way of working of each committee. While major structural review should be relatively infrequent, say every five years, there is a case for each committee having at least an agenda review each year. This should cover

▽   What has been on the agenda that need not have been on the agenda?
▽   What should have been on the agenda that was not on the agenda?
▽   How much of the agenda has been concerned with the running of departments (the production process) and how much with the problems to be met (the marketing process)?
▽   Do the form of reports assist ready understanding?

If the committee is an instrument to be used, it has to be retuned regularly to ensure it meets councillors' needs. Each committee should 'pause' to consider its way of working.

The differentiated cycle

It has been argued that the committee is based on the assumption that control should be exercised as it happens. It is expressed in the undifferentiated cycle, in which meetings take place at regular intervals, without distinguishing the purpose of one meeting from another. Strategy may even be considered as merely another item on a lengthy agenda.

The new requirements challenge the undifferentiated cycle. The requirements of learning, direction and review may best be met by a differentiated cycle. Thus a committee which had ten routine meetings a year could reduce those to five through an agenda review, but could schedule separate meetings to consider

▽   changes in the environment, needs met and needs unmet — learning
▽   the strategy of the committee and its main policies — direction
▽   performance in relation to policies and strategy — review.

In addition two more additional meetings could be scheduled, each to consider a particular policy issue in depth.

A differentiated cycle gives expression to the new management required by local government, creating organisational 'pauses' in which the committee can control the working of the authority in accordance with its political purposes.

Relating processes to political direction

It is not sufficient to constitute a differentiated cycle, the processes within that cycle must enable political direction. One of the purposes of regular re-appraisal is to establish whether the management processes present issues and supply information that meet political needs. That can only be determined by the councillors themselves, but organisational time and space have to be created for its consideration.

Two examples can be highlighted. The first is whether the management processes of the authority take account of the political manifesto of the majority party where there is one (or indeed of all parties in the hung situation). It is not the case that manifestos can or should be translated automatically into management action. Commitments in manifestos are rarely tied into the circumstances of the authority. That does not lessen the possibility of using them, but rather increases the importance of their use to explore the interaction between political and management processes.

The second example is the form in which strategic and policy issues are presented to committees. Often these are put forward at a level of generality that makes it difficult for councillors to test proposals against particular cases. Indeed attempts by councillors to do so may be felt by officers to be evading the issue. 'All they will ever discuss is particular cases'. Yet it is in their effect on particular cases that strategy and policy gain their impact. The natural flow of policy discussion is consideration of general policy — consideration of its particular impact — reconsideration of policy.

That is not a retreat from policy discussion but, rather, its effective expression. Policy and management processes must be designed for councillors, rather than councillors be fitted into policy and management processes designed for officers.

New settings for new roles

The main setting normally provided for the councillors' role is the traditional service or central committee meeting. The agenda, the table, the room, the seating arrangements dictate a way of doing business. The business that had to be done was authoritative decision-making required by the ongoing process of administration. The setting fitted the role. But the setting does not fit learning, direction and review; nor does it fit the exploration of policy issues in depth or fit the identification of needs and problems faced by the authority. Different settings are required for different purposes.

Different forms of committee and forums for discussion are emerging: — area committees, womens committees, management boards for specific purposes, working parties, panels and seminars used to explore new issues. It is important that these new developments are clearly related to an authoritative decision-making structure. If that is not secured, then discussion and action are separated in frustration. The differentiated cycle provides a means of distinguishing settings within the working of committees themselves. While routine meetings can follow the pre-determined patterns, other meetings can escape from the agenda and the formalities of decision-making. Settings can aid discussion or can confine it.

New models beyond the present

The traditional working of the local authority is based on the principle that the council is responsible for all that happens in the authority. It is, in effect, both the legislative and the executive. The council delegates its executive role but remains responsible for all that is done in its name. We have become so accustomed to this principle that it is often assumed to be a necessary feature of local government.

Yet most other countries in Western Europe draw a distinction between the council and the political executive. The political executive may be an Executive Board constituted by the council from its own membership. It may be an individual appointed by the council or directly elected by the whole area of the authority.

It is at present impossible for a local authority to adopt such models because it cannot itself remove the responsibility placed upon it by law. Such alternative models have a role, however, in opening up consideration of the principles on which local authorities are constituted. Local authorities could work towards such models, even if they could not fully achieve them or if they fear the concentration of power would develop alternatives. Past patterns should not be assumed to be fixed even in law. In a period of challenge and change, change in the organisational model may become possible and the road to experiment opened up if authorities seek it.

The new significance of the representative role

The representative role of the councillor has received little recognition in the workings of most authorities. At its most basic this is to do with the representation of constituents and a particular geographical area in the affairs of the council. It is also to do with the representation of the council's collective interest back in the community. The enabling role as the expression of local government gives a new importance to that role. The enabling role will depend on councillors who are both the expression of community *voice* in government and the means of community *choice*. It will require the development of the representative role to its full potential.

A voice for the community

It is through the council that needs and problems faced in an area can gain expression. The council can be and has been a means of expressing the concerns of the local community. Many councils have protested against the closure of a local hospital or of a local railway line. Most councils shared the concern of their community about growing unemployment and the state of the local economy. The council whether county or district, metropolitan or shire, is elected to represent those who live within its area. As the number of public and private agencies involved in the life of the community increases so there is a fragmentation of the process of government and a growth in the number of bodies not directly responsible to the local electorate. The local authority is the only body at local level which can legitimately speak on behalf of local people within this fragmented structure of community government.

The council can speak on behalf of its community, but it is not structured to do so. It is structured around the services it provides and the procedures which dominate its working reflect the requirements of those services. Time and space, therefore, need to be found and forums created where issues which are broader than the working of particular services can be considered. The focus needs to be changed from one that is inward on the organisation of service to one which is outward to the community.

It is not just a business of creating the right structures and procedures for the role to be played out, it is also a matter of ensuring that the councillor has access to the right information. Councillors will need to have as wide a range of information as possible about the community and what is happening to it. This will include data about needs and how they might be met and an assessment of current provision in the community; market research in the broadest sense. They also need to have access, for example, to the range of organisations which go to make up the community's collective life and whose voice needs to be heard.

Building the community strategy

It has been shown that it is not enough for the enabling council simply to have a strategy for its own services, nor is it enough for a local authority to give expression to the needs, problems and opportunities faced by a community. It should go beyond this and assist the development of a community strategy, which shows how those needs and problems can be overcome and opportunities realised. In effect a community strategy sets goals for the local community and for the local authority within it. The council cannot impose such a strategy on others. The goals that it sets, if they are to be effective, must be more than its own. They must carry the commitment of others upon whom their success depends. Councillors will, therefore, have to develop strategy through interaction with all those concerned with the development of the area. It will be the role of those councillors who have a particular interest in thinking and working strategically to lead in finding ways of bringing the whole range of interests into the process. Other councillors who have more limited concerns but legitimately represent their part of the community should also be able to express them in the process.

A community strategy cannot and should not pre-determine the actions of organisations and individuals in detail. The community strategy will not be all-embracing, but selective—highlighting, identifying and revealing key issues and problems, but never over-determining—even for the authority's own actions. It may focus on an area such as the inner city or on the problems of rural villages. It may focus on a group, such as the growing numbers of the vulnerable elderly; or it may highlight issues of environmental concern.

A community strategy will not be found in the workings of service committees nor will it be found inside the organisation of the authority alone. It has to be broadly based and developed through and with others. To be successful in this the council has to strive for a strategy for the community that goes beyond the services it provides, and it has to develop settings in which councillors can explore the nature of that strategy with other organisations and individuals within their communities. The councillors are the link with their communities.

Community action

A strategy by itself is of little use unless it leads to action. The council has to learn ways by which it can facilitate action without itself necessarily being directly involved in that action as well as securing that its own actions help to achieve the community strategy. The issue for councillors, as for officers, is to realise that the resources the authority possesses, which are usually bound up in the direct provision of services or in established processes of regulation and inspection, can have a wider role. Information, skills, powers, staff, and money are conventionally treated as belonging to a service and to the committee which controls them. Councillors need to recognise that these can have a wider use as the means of leverage for community action.

The councillor has to have the means of grasping the totality of resources which can be available if the potential is to be realised. The council needs to develop the capacity to manage the deployment of its resources for community action as well as for the services it is directly providing. This will give new importance to the role of the policy and resources committee or its equivalent as the place within the structure of the council where attention can be focused on this wider resources issue. Ways then need to be found of relating internal resources to the wider range available in the community.

Networks of influence and learning

Councillors are and should be part of the networks that link the local authority to the organisations, groups and individuals from whom the enabling council must learn and with whom they must work in action and in influence. These networks need to be enhanced, extended and maintained. Much is already in place. For example, all councils appoint councillors as their representatives on a wide range of outside bodies, advisory committees or consultative bodies. They have in effect laid the basis for a network of influence and learning.

A network for influence and learning is only of value if it is used. A network of inter-organisational relationships that is not used by the local authority exists in isolation, serving no purpose for local government beyond the multiplication of meetings. Councillors appointed to outside bodies are rarely briefed and are not usually expected or required to report back, over-loaded agendas of committees having no place for such niceties. External representation may sometimes be interesting but it does not have a valued place in the life of the council. This needs to change. It will increasingly provide a useful means of learning and of influence.

The community monitor

The councillor as representative for an area has a key role in monitoring and in learning. In surgeries, in letters and in informal contacts the councillor is a means of contact between the council and its community. The public in their contacts with councillors raise many issues about and beyond the services for which it is responsible. The public treat the councillor as their representative and from that both council and councillor can learn. The councillor can be a monitor on action taken or not taken in the area and an inspector of quality, who can contribute to contract and services monitoring. He or she is a channel for complaints and for the soft data of ideas, suggestions and awareness of what is going on.

Despite its obvious importance, and the satisfaction it gives to many councillors, the organisation of most local authorities gives little or no recognition to the role and to the concern of councillors for their area. Indeed, councillors interested in their areas are often seen as 'purely parochial'. The exception has been local authorities which have set up area committees creating a setting in which the role of the councillor as representative is legitimatised and given support. These are forums in which any issues relevant to that area can be raised and a setting in which the role of community monitor can be developed. Their lessons need to be learned in other parts of the council's life.

The advocate for the citizen

The councillor represents an area and those who live within it. The individual citizens can look to the councilor as their representative. The councillor is the advocate to whom the citizens can turn to represent them both in dealing with the local authority and also with other agencies. This work is a vital part of the representative role. A citizen is entitled to representation and does not recognise the boundaries of local authority services as being the outer limits of that entitlement.

The role of the councillor as advocate for the citizen needs to be developed to reflect and express the wide ranging concern of the local authority as local government. It is obviously further extended where, as may often happen, advocacy on behalf of individuals becomes advocacy on behalf of the local area. In fulfilling the role of advocate the councillor will again need support and advice from the council's organisation. It is another role which is not new but one which is too often under valued by the formal organisation of the local authority.

New structures and processes

Structures and processes will have to be found which give recognition to the many roles of the councillor. Those which focus only on the provision of service give inadequate expression to local government. The possibilities are many and individual councils will need to experiment and work with those that best suit their situation. They include:

▽   review of the committee structure to release time and capacity to play new roles

▽   changes to the committee structure to allow it to reflect wider community issues and interests outside the straitjacket of service provision

▽   the creation of management boards in place of committees where quick
      and effective action is required

Bolton Metropolitan District has carried out an agenda analysis as
part of a Decision Making experiment. The analysis showed that
agendas were made up as follows:
Class 1 20 per cent of decisions were of a policy nature
Class 2 57 per cent were of an executive nature
Class 3 13 per cent were of an inter-face nature concerning our rela-
          tionship with outside organisations
Class 4 10 per cent were information items. Each of these classes
          were further analysed into sub-categories. The review provid-
          ed the opportunity to consider whether appropriate business
          was going to committees and sub committees. (Bolton 1987)

▽   the development of the differentiated cycle for committees, reducing
      the number of routine meetings and providing organisational space in
      the cycle of meeting for consideration of strategy, policy-making, effec-
      tiveness review and quality monitoring meetings constituted for those
      purposes

Avon County Council has introduced a committee system designed
to separate
(a) policy making — the setting down of principles within which the
      affairs of the council are managed or executed
(b) policy implementation — management or executive action
      required to comply with or give effort to policy
(c) review of policy or implementation (Avon 1987) — each of which
      is made the responsibility of a separate sub-committee that can
      then develop its own way of working

Clywd County Council has reviewed its committee structures and
also the method of working of the committees and operational decisions are the responsibility of sub-committees, while the main committees have only three meetings per year, each of which concentrates
on one aspect of the management process : strategy, budgetting and
review. At the same time the role of the councillors is also given
expression in panels and working parties.

▽   the development of committees to support the representative role of
      the councillor
▽   organisational support for the role of the councillor as a representative
      of the local authority on external organisations and adequate channels
      to tie this back into the rest of the authority
▽   a support unit for the role of councillor as citizen

> Birmingham City Council has set up 12 area committees consisting of the elected councillors for the wards in the area and the MP for the constituency. They are held in the area and the public are encouraged to attend and to raise issues. Although given few powers they provide an opportunity for local councillors to consider issues affecting their area. They ensure that issues of concern to people in an area are placed on the agenda of service committees and the area committees views considered and replied to. They introduce an areal perspective into the working of the council.

▽ better systems for the handling of enquiries, complaints and suggestions and support for the maintenance of councillors' 'surgeries'

▽ better information systems for use both by councillors and the community

▽ better resourced support and secretarial arrangements for all councillors.

> Blyth Valley District Council built up a management development programme for councillors, with councillors themselves trained to act as management development advisers for other councillors. As the leader argued 'After all, we cannot remain aloof from the management process without suffering criticism of our capacity to govern through the council'. (LGTB)

▽ the council meeting constituted as the 'state of the community' forum in which councillors are joined by individuals and representatives of other organisations to focus on the key problems and issues facing the community

▽ similar processes which bring in others in the community and allow for the preparation of a community strategy as a framework for action by the council and other organisations

▽ the investigative panel in which councillors, along with representatives of other organisations, probe a key issue facing an area

▽ the Green Paper in which the council sets out proposals for wide ranging community debate as to how a problem should be handled perhaps culminating in an open forum

▽ the appointment of councillors as spokespersons on topics of council concern and providing them with organisational support

▽ wider use of working parties and panels to promote joint working in the development of ideas and policy and in the monitoring of action

▽ the creation of networks of organisations concerned with particular community concerns with councillors as local authority representatives

▽ the redefinition of the role of policy and resources committees as a focus for the council's contribution to the community strategy and the broker of resources for community action.

These possibilities illustrate how the organisation of the authority can support the roles of the councillor in the general management of the authority. Effective general management requires the full development of the councillors policy and management roles and the recognition within the working of the authority of the councillors representative role. For general management supports the role of local authorities as local government and effective local government requires an effective political process. This book's contention is that this cannot be achieved in the traditional working of the committee system. Once the assumed necessity of past practice is challenged, as it is by current developments, then new settings and processes can be established to support the roles of the councillor. Local authorities in building general management cannot restrict their actions to development of the role of officers. It is the councillors who distinguish local authorities as local government. Having said this, it is of course also critical that the officer world is developed for general management.

6 Developing changing officer roles

Key points

▲ *As local government changes so change is necessary in the roles required of officers leading to a new management*

▲ *The development of this new management cannot be based on the professional role alone but must be about general management*

▲ *If general management is to be built for local government then management development must be geared to this end*

▲ *Management development must itself be part of a wider approach to human resource management if local authorities are to achieve their full potential as local government*

Changing the inheritance

The developments outlined require a reconsideration of many of the roles played by officers. Some of these are more clearly and quickly changing than others, but few are untouched. For example

▽ The role of the client is being separated from that of contractor. Managers on each side have a new definition of their job, with officers who have been used to both controlling what is required and its provision now being required to focus on their separate roles.

▽ In education departments, the role of advisers is being reviewed, just as that of the professional engaged in educational administration is under the microscope as the relationship between the authority and its schools changes.

▽ Central support departments are increasingly working as contractors to meet the needs of their colleagues in service departments and organisations.

▽ The re-definition of the centre in the sense of clarifying the strategic planning and management responsibility of the authority is changing the role of the chief executives, chief officers and the relevant support functions.

▽ The legislation implementing the Griffiths proposals on Community Care will lead to new roles for managers in social services.

▽ The emphasis on the public as customers and citizens changes the roles of many officers right across local government's services.

Conventional training, usually deeply rooted in the variety of professions which dominate the local government service and with little formal recognition of management training and development, seems far removed from these new demands and concerns. But the reconsideration of roles is not due to legislative change alone or even to the new emphasis on the customer. It it also the consequence of the wider changes in the environment within which local government is set.

Many of these changes have already been touched upon. Two need re-emphasising here. The first is changing ideas about management itself. Understanding of the ways in which organisations work best and of the process of management has become more sophisticated. Reinforced by the advance of technology on the one hand and by general thinking about how best to put management emphasis on the responsive delivery of services on the other, management responsibility and accountability has been pushed downwards. This has forced the explicit definition of the managerial content of jobs often sharpening the differences with conventional professional practice.

The second, which will become progressively more important over the next few years, is the consequence of demographic change. The shortage of skills in a number of professional and geographical areas has already underlined the importance of managing positively the people resource of the local authority. These difficulties will be compounded as structural change works its way through the labour market. Between 1988 and 1993 there will have been an almost 25 per cent reduction in the number of young people entering the labour market.

The 1980s placed an emphasis on the careful management of maney as public expenditure was constrained. The 1990s will place an emphasis on the management of people. Together they will have sharpened the need for good management overall.

Demographic change is being met by some authorities with a pay cheque response. Pay and conditions are seen as the best 'fix'. Many others have recognised that the problem is too big for this and demands a more imaginative response. The design of organisations and jobs, the importance of the right level of culture and other determinants of job satisfaction, and challenging professional restrictive practices which require unproven levels of qualification to discharge jobs capable of being 'de-professionalised' all need attention. Equalities issues and opportunities can be brought centre stage as possibilities emerge for a growing role for people who have been grossly under-represented in many local government jobs.

Imaginative solutions require imaginative management and imaginative management needs to be rooted in management and organisation development which has an eye to the future and not to the past. At the centre of this are the changing roles of managers; not just in the way they have changed over recent years but the way in which they will go on changing.

In Chapter 2 it was argued that what is required if local government is to effectively respond to the challenges faced, is a development of general management. That development must effect both the role of managers, the processes of management, especially of human resource management, and of management development. Above all, it must reflect a shift away from the dominance of the professional.

A challenge to the professional monopoly

In the traditional administration of local authorities, the dominant task was the direct provision of services on a predetermined pattern, which was largely set by professional practise. The dominant roles were not seen as management roles, but as professional ones. As ideas about management have developed, they have been about the stewardship of resources within a professional and service framework.

The professional is concerned to maintain professional standards, to develop professional skills and to extend professional knowledge. The reference point is the wider profession and the professional leader will often play a role in that arena, encouraging staff in their professional development. These are natural emphases, for example, for a chief officer and others who have reached senior professional positions in the department, and for whom, identity with the profession has been a driving force and provided qualification for the most senior job.

The emphasis on the role of the professional leader has had great strengths and has been at the heart of the tradition of local government administration. It has given a guarantee of standards and the promise of expertise and skill in its application. The professionalism of a department has traditionally been a hallmark of its performance. Professional identity, however, has often led to a narrow focus for the officer's role which has eschewed many of the perspectives demanded of the contemporary manager.

In many ways the crucial test of the officer's job has come to be *management*. The professional approach too often assumes an organisation runs itself; which simply met the requirements of local administration. An organisation that merely runs itself will lose purpose and direction and will not support the role of local government in a changing environment. For that management is required to enable the organisation to achieve new purposes and direction.

In the management of the organisation:

▽   the changing environment has to be understood
▽   the direction of management action has to be set
▽   resources have to be obtained, deployed and guided
▽   work procedures have to be organised
▽   organisation has to be built, watched, and adapted
▽   organisational control has to be developed
▽   organisational learning has to be fostered
▽   organisational impact and action have to be monitored.

Those are not roles for the professional alone, the officer charged with organisational responsibilities has to be an effective manager.

More than professional advice is required

Senior officers have combined professionalism with the role of adviser to council and committee. The officer does not take decisions on policy, or so convention and form would have us believe. Decisions on policy, and often on practice, are taken by council or committee. It is only when the decisions have been made with appropriate formality and recorded that decisions are said to have been made. The officer advises; that is the form. Reality may be different. Advice on policy can easily become the making of policy; information and recommendation by an officer can have a powerful impact.

Though form dictates that the officer advises the committee, for many the reality may well be that the officer advises the party in control of the council. The most important advice may even be that given only to the chair of the committee. Policy often emerges in the coming together of advice and decisions outside committee meetings. Yet form still has an influence on reality. Reports from the officers are given to the committee. The officer is the person who is there to advise it. Form often gains most reality in the hung situation. If no party can guarantee a majority, then decisions must lie with the committee or the council beyond it.

Advice has conventionally been drawn from the world and ideas of the profession. These have been tempered by administrative convenience and local colour. Increasingly, however, officers are required to deliver a blend of professional and managerial advice. The stewardship and development of financial and human resources has become more and more important. Advice is never simple. The professional and the manager have to blend their perspectives together. Above all, advice must be grounded in political understanding which does not mean political commitment. It is the politically unaware officer who is most likely to show political bias in misunderstanding. The management task in local government is to support and express the legitimate political process and that requires political understanding.

The corporate role

Each officer is a member of a part of the organisation and will identify with that part. However, if the local authority is to achieve its role as local government, the various parts of the organisation must relate together. Many of the major issues which the local authority has to deal with or which are of serious concern to the local community do not respect internal boundaries between departments or operating units.

For some officers a corporate role is of great importance, extending both the personal contribution and the departmental role. In the corporate working of the authority, the officer faces wider community issues over and above those on which the department focuses.

Some people seem to believe that corporate involvement need only be the preserve of the chief officer board or management team. Corporate working should not be restricted in this way; if it is, it will have failed in its impact. An officer is engaged in corporate working in advice given and in working groups, in managing a corporate activity or in the day-to-day work of management, but with a perspective that extends beyond the department.

In dealing with corporate issues, an officer should not be expected to abandon a departmental or even a professional perspective. Rather the officer should be encouraged to apply the perspective to the wider issues. Corporate management can extend rather than limit the capacity of departments and of those who work in them. The wider corporate perspective, unbounded by a narrower professionalism, is an important part of general management. Involvement in corporate activities is an important way of developing general management competence through experience.

There is a special additional responsibility which falls on chief officers. Increasingly, through a corporate involvement, they are expected to assume a strategic leadership role in the authority. The chief officers, together with the chief executive and whatever support they define, are emerging as a new 'centre'. In this there is the responsibility to work with the politicians in the definition of strategy, to ensure that the organisation and its staff are geared up to the implementation of strategy and to manage the processes which deliver that strategy.

Departmental, corporate and strategic management roles all require different approaches, understanding and skills to the traditional professional roles. The fact that the roles do not always sit comfortably together and have to be constantly rediscovered in the balance further sharpens the abilities that are needed. It will also be clear that the balance between them is also being changed by many of the developments have discussed. The enabling concept with its emphasis on building networks and managing complex relationships, exemplifies the point best. The old model makes no sense in this context. The ability to operate across boundaries and to manage strategically is at a premium. Traditional administration based on the primacy of professionalism is being replaced by general management.

The role of the chief executives

In the midst of these changes the position of the chief executive is critical. The chief executive is at the hub of the authority, at a point of multiple interactions. The chief executive's role is made and re-made in the many relationships that are formed in those interactions.

The chief executive has key relationships with the political leadership and the council generally, with the external world of agencies and organisations, with the chief officers both individually and collectively, with the authority's organisation and with the community it serves. It is the interaction between these relationships that conditions the role, for it is the chief executive's role to manage the relationship between

▽   the political structure and the officer structure;
▽   the different departments of the authority;
▽   the external environment and the internal environment of the authority;

while recognising that these relationships cannot be managed by one individual alone. In managing and being managed by the complex of relationships, chief executives require organisational understanding that goes beyond the particular incident or event that will inevitably occupy their time and energy.

However, to define the role by relationships alone is not sufficient. The management of relationships only is not sufficient. The management of relationships gains meaning in purpose. If the argument of this book is correct, that purpose should be found in the role of local authorities as local government. It has been argued that that role creates the need for general management. That being the case, the chief executive's role is the development and maintenance of general management, recognising that management itself must change and develop. For as it has been shown the task is not the management of change but the management of transformation. The chief executive's role is developed in general management just as much as it is about guiding and developing such management.

The skills and attitudes of general management

All of this emphasises the need, already argued, for a different kind of manager throughout the organisation. The changes point to the emergence of a new breed of managers who have more in common than they are divided by disciplinary or organisational boundaries.

Any management needs to be grounded in the special purposes and conditions of its organisational or service context. Local authorities have allowed this necessity to be exaggerated by professional apprenticeship and professional identity, insisting, almost without exception, that particular professional practice and loyalty is a prerequisite for a senior management job. They have bolstered this by maintaining sets of departmental (and committee) boundaries which enclose those professional groups. Above all, these boundaries have then been further reinforced by careers and experience confined within them.

The new balance which now needs to be struck is one which allows managers to recognise the special characteristics and purposes of particular services but breaks down the boundaries which separate them. The general themes of management in the local authority need to be recognised as being as important as the particular. Over the next few years, regardless of professional, service and departmental boundaries, new skills and styles of management must be developed. From what has already been said it will be clear that in the place of professionals presiding over the direct delivery of their service, local government needs managers:

▽ who are able to take as broad and unfettered a view as possible
▽ who recognise that the local authorities can act in a wide variety of ways in direct provision and on indirect action or influence
▽ who are skilled in the business of influencing, of understanding organisational and people development, and of coping with paradox and uncertainty
▽ who are entrepreneurial in the sense of constantly looking for opportunities to innovate and find new ways of working to improve the effectiveness of the organisation
▽ who have the skills required to manage contracts and the abilities to achieve them and who recognise that local government requires political direction and needs to manage with political sensitivity and awareness.

Managers, across all disciplines, will also need to be equipped more completely with the skills which allow them to operate with greater freedom, responsibility and discretion in achieving political purpose.

The skills and attitudes required of managers need to match the circumstances in which they operate. Obviously those required of an enabling council will extend beyond those required for the management of direct service provision, just as an emphasis on closeness to customer and citizen will require particular characteristics or the management of a direct service organisation will demand a style conversant with a contract culture.

Recent national work in conjunction with the Forum for Management Education and Development has identified four broad classifications of management competences. These are a helpful way of thinking about the basic requirements of management and are beginning to be used widely in local government.

1.   Competences relating to dealing with *people*:

▽   those for whom one has responsibility
▽   peers
▽   those to whom one reports
▽   clients, customers and citizens.

2.   Competences concerned with *managing activities*

▽   financial activities
▽   systems control
▽   techniques
▽   functional activities.

3.   Competences reflecting a *sensitivity to environment* with respect to:

▽   the political world
▽   customer expectations/needs
▽   legal considerations
▽   organisational, social, economic and technological change.

4.   Competences reflecting *personal effectiveness*:

▽   communication
▽   numeracy and the use of numerical techniques
▽   people orientation
▽   results orientation
▽   self-awareness/development orientation.

Just as traditional management in the local authority was grounded in competences derived from professionalism and from the assumptions of self-sufficiency and of direct provision, so general management will require its own competences. The example of the enabling role can mean that there is a move away from the management *action* to a more subtle set of concerns to do with:

▽   influence
▽   the building of alliances, co-operation or consensus
▽   less certainty

and the *processes* which underpin them. The differences in content, approach and style should not be underestimated. Using the above grouping of competences one can say that managers need to be adept in:

1   **People**

▽   The art of persuasion
▽   The management of influencing

▽   Building relationships for multi-organisational teams
▽   Negotiation skills with different types of organisation

2   **Managing activities**

▽   Skills in contract management
▽   Forms of financial analysis appropriate to a multi-disciplinary situation
▽   Indirect management

3   **Sensitivity to environment**

▽   Organisational understanding of those with whom the authority has to work
▽   Networking skills across a range of organisations
▽   Community monitoring

4   **Personal effectiveness**

▽   Tolerance of organisational uncertainty
▽   Readiness to adopt different modes of working
▽   A capacity for learning and development
▽   An innovative capacity

What has been shown for the enabling role could also be shown for the specific task of contract management or for the more general requirements of closeness to the public as customer and citizen.

Understanding the competences required helps to understand what is involved in the development of general management. The competences must not be seen, however, as a series of isolated requirements separate from each other. They must be grounded in the totality of the general management task for local government.

Building the capacity for general management

If the capacity for general management is to be built, there are major challenges to be met in the short term:

▽   As we have just shown there is a need to be clearer about what is wanted of managers and what their key competences should be, and of how those competences are related to general management for local government.
▽   A multitude of ways need to be found which will expose managers of one discipline to the concerns of another. This may be achieved by career moves across organisational boundaries, by secondment or by involvement in multi-disciplinary project work. Such things happen at the moment but to a limited extent and not as part of a planned policy to widen experience and understanding.
▽   There will also be a need to examine management recruitment patterns and the transition from professional practice to management responsibility. Is there a role for the management trainee? What is the best point to envisage a move away from the base professional discipline? Should there be a 'fast track' and so on?
▽   The under-representation of some groups (notably women and members of ethnic minority communities) in management presents a prob-

lem and an opportunity. A problem because there are relatively few of them in post; an opportunity because they could provide a pool of people free of many of the restraints of conventional models and folk-ways.

▽   The need to encourage and oil the wheels of change by promoting wide debate and general appreciation of the implications of what is currently happening in local government not merely for the present but for the future. Although this may sound self-evident, it is a serious issue. The danger is that each change is treated in isolation and that the short-term necessities of preparation predominate. The more immediate pressures and the more traumatic the current change, the more difficult it is to stand back and get a sense of perspective about the future and about what needs to be done to change the nature of management for the 1990s.

▽   Above all there is a need not only to put new emphasis on management development but also to put the spotlight on the development of new management practice and to find ways of sharing it. The development of managers and of management practice go hand-in-hand; they need to be associated with the development of the organisation.

DEVELOPING MANAGERS AND MANAGEMENT

It takes more than an understanding of what is needed in terms of organisation design, management style or competences to ensure that they are successfully put into place. Development does not just happen. A local authority needs to have strategies for developing the organisation to ensure that it is capable of meeting and delivering the direction which has been set

> Cambridgeshire County Council has undertaken a re-shaping of the organisation to achieve a strategy based on a commitment to 'clear management objectives and accountability for results'. This has entailed amongst other development
>
> ▽   'the introduction of performance management to maximise individuals' performance and develop their potential
> ▽   the introduction of new pay practices to match the newly evaluated jobs
> ▽   the introduction of a management development programme.
>
> Also being developed are
>
> ▽   more sophisticated pay practices linked with performances
> ▽   support mechanisms to help individual plan and manage their own careers and to help the council with succession planning
> ▽   the concept of renewable contracts for chief officers.' (LGTB, 1989).

for it. Within this there needs also to be a related strategy for management development to ensure that staff develop as specialist and general managers to fulfil the roles required.

Rochdale Metropolitan District is committed to 'improve services against a background of declining resources'. It recognises that this can only be achieved by its staff. 'Consequently greater emphasis needs to be given to *training* in the authority. Politicians, managers and employees at all levels need to develop new skills. Training must be targeted, of good quality and relevant to the individuals and the organisation's needs. Thorough monitoring systems need to be established to ensure:

(i)   that the training is reaching members and staff at all levels;
(ii) that it is responding to identified demand.

Furthermore, if staff are going to give their commitment to the council, managers must:

▽   keep staff well informed of new/planned initiatives
▽   treat career development seriously
▽   encourage a team approach to problem solving'. (Rochdale, 1989)

Strategies then need to be translated into action. Organisations and people do not change just because strategies have been defined and new sets of values adopted. A careful programme of action needs to be set. It can be opportunistic and implemented in a piecemeal kind of way but only if the strategy is clear. The failure in the past has been to try to achieve change in an ad hoc way *without* any clear direction or framework.

There is no one right way of achieving the task. Management development can take place in a number of different ways. Traditionally, people have instinctively thought of management courses but it can also take place through

▽   the variety of working experiences
▽   counselling and guidance
▽   career moves
▽   job exchanges
▽   project work
▽   action learning
▽   group discussion
▽   use of distance learning
▽   reading
▽   listening and reflection.

The key point is that all these activities should be understood as part of management development, and be related to the needs both of the individual and the organisation.

This will only happen if the authority has an effective management development strategy which follows the principles laid down in the Local Government Training Board's publication *Going for Better Management*. It must:

▽   'Make explicit the authority's real commitment to the training and development of managers (and members) at all levels.
▽   Highlight from the authority's strategy the key changes (such as those

affecting service delivery, performance, and style) that have management development implications.

▽ Outline an effective system for identifying the development needs of individual managers in relation to those changes, to current issues and problems, and their own needs.

▽ Make provision for every manager to take an active responsibility for his/her own development.

▽ Clarify the roles and responsibilities of those within the authority (from chief executive to management development adviser) and those outside the authority (from educational institutions to management consultants).

▽ Make explicit the core management competences required by managers at different levels within the organisation.

▽ Have clear processes and objectives for the selection of managers.

▽ Make provision for career succession and planning.

▽ Outline an effective system for (a) assessing managerial potential, (b) reviewing the performance of all staff.

▽ Provide a systematic and integrated plan of on and off-the-job management education and development, shaped to meet the needs of both individual and organisation.' (LGTB, 1988a)

Essex County Council have developed a programme of internal and external secondments. The purposes include

▽ 'to provide an individual with skills/knowledge/contacts needed in a particular work area

▽ to provide new ideas/concepts for the county council

▽ to create some movement in a static work force.'

Human Resource Management

General management requires not only management development but human resource management, because it is concerned with using the full potential of those who work within the authority. There are few people in local government whose jobs will not be affected by the changes which are discussed at the start of this book. Broad personnel policies and, in particular, the specifics of training and development need to be geared to producing a highly competent, flexible and committed workforce to ensure effective performance. The book in this series, *Human Resource Management in Local Government* by Alan Fowler, discusses the themes in more depth. What that shows to be important is that the following kinds of issues should be faced:

▽ Traditional patterns of recruitment and selection may not meet the needs of the times or the exigencies of demographic structure. Imaginative approaches are needed to fit working conditions to new realities.

▽ Staff appraisal and development is part of the learning process both for the authority and for the individual.

▽ Payments systems are breaking out of the bounds set by past practice,
   but motivation cannot be achieved by payments systems alone.
▽ The developing role of local authorities requires communication along
   many channels for both councillors and officers. The authority must
   create a new capacity for informing but also for listening.

> In Cumbria County Council, which is a hung authority, the three
> political leaders have agreed upon a statement to all employees which
> sets out 'their vision of the future direction and approach at the coun-
> cil'. It stresses that the 'political, financial and social environment in
> which we operate has shifted during the 1980s, and traditional
> assumptions about the role of local government have been chal-
> lenged. Increasingly the trend is for local councils to adopt an
> enabling role, rather than one which is exclusively as a provider.'
> (Cumbria, 1989). It sets out the direction for organisational develop-
> ment based on public service, business planning, managerial free-
> dom, more internal business units, customer care quality and good
> internal communication.

> Enfield London Borough, in their Corporate Identity launch issued
> by the chief executive, stressed that 'Each manager and supervisor is a
> centre of communication' and went on to stress 'The council looks
> for excellence and appropriateness in what is transmitted and
> received. Employees should know the strategies and intentions of the
> council, their department and their role. They should have systematic
> appraisal to know how they are doing and training and development
> to meet their needs. Above all communication should be two way.
> Anyone working for Enfield should have a genuine opportunity to
> change and influence their environment and working conditions.'
> (Enfield, 1989).

▽ Equal opportunity is a necessary condition of general management,
   because without it the authority is a flawed organisation because it has
   not realised its full potential.
▽ Effective general management requires patterns of industrial relations
   that recognise the authority will be a changing organisation, but that
   change can be built with and through trade unions.

The agenda of human resources management is thus an agenda for general
management. People are local government's key resource. Changing the
way they are developed and enabled to contribute to their authorities is as
fundamental a part of managing change as any. However, management
development and human resource development have to be set within an
overall response to change. Above all they have to be driven by the need to
develop the new roles required by the holistic approach to management.

7 Getting the balance right

Key points

▲ *Management in local government is changing and not just because of legislative change. The external environment and trends in management thinking have their own impact*

▲ *Yet the dominance of legislative change can create imbalance, building strength but neglecting critical issues*

▲ *An emphasis on competitive and contractual arrangements has been prompted by the legislation. It has sharpened management but cannot be all-embracing*

▲ *A commercial culture is not enough for government. A competitive council has also to be a co-operative council*

▲ *The task is to build be a new balance in management for local government — and for that a holistic approach is required. This is a pre-requuisite for general management.*

The challenge restated

This book has set out the changes required if the management of local authorities is to meet the challenge of the 1990s. Those challenges mean that local authorities have to be capable of changing their activities and their way of working in relation to a changing environment. It calls for a new management that focuses on of this changing environment and on the changes required from local government, rather than on the continuous provision of services on a pre-determined pattern. It calls for local authorities to develop their role as local government rather than local administration, for that is the meaning of the enabling role put forward in Chapter 1. It is a challenge for councillors and officers alike.

That the management of local government is changing is beyond doubt, but it is changing often more in response to central government legislation, than it is to the wider challenges of the 1990s. While the government's legislation is in part a response to those challenges itself, it is not by itself an adequate response. The danger is that if the response is only to the legislation there will be an imbalance in the management of local authorities, which will prevent them achieving their full potential as local government.

The danger is all the more real because of local government's well-developed facility to rise to the occasion and to tackle and solve problems which get in its way. The energy and innovation which has been the hall-mark of the response to CCT, and to the housing and education legislation, and which will doubtless characterise the shaping of the Griffiths reform in the social services is typical of a long tradition. Creditable as this is it can often produce a single-mindedness of purpose. This single-mindedness can easily lead to losing sight of the wood for the trees. The relationships between changes, and more important, trends in the wider environment become obscured in the rush to get the immediate problems solved.

Chapter 1 also pointed out that society and its expectations are changing and will go on doing so. Technological changes bring new opportunities and much of local government has only just begun to come to terms with their implications. Demographic change not only impacts on the nature of services required but is beginning to present profound issues for organisation and management as the reduced number of young people entering the labour market begins to bite. Even without the legislation local authorities were beginning to review and reconstruct their relationships with their public — as both service users and citizens. Wider trends in management practice and changing understanding of the most effective way to run organisations cannot be ignored. And so the catalogue continues. The task is to recognise and meet all the strands or change.

Direct and indirect effects of legislative changes

The effect of central government legislation on the management of local authorities, is both direct and indirect. The direct effects of the legislation are well known to everyone in local government.

The cumulative direct effect of all these changes has been to challenge the assumption of self-sufficiency and the consequential necessity of organising for direct provision. For many areas of its responsibilities the local authority has had to change from direct management to indirect management or from control as it happens to control through contracts or other arrangements. This book has shown that these are fundamental changes in the working of local authorities. Even where legislation has not required the same degree of management change as, say CCT (compulsory competitive tendering) or in education, it has been a catalyst in forcing a reconsideration of new ways of working.

The indirect effects of the legislation can be as important as the direct effects and they are not limited to the legislation discussed. Indirect effects can be seen in:

▽　the way in which the requirements of competitive tendering have led to the growth of semi-contractual arrangements, such as service level agreements, to govern the relationships between different parts of the authority and, in particular, between the central departments (Treasurers, Personnel, Legal, etc.) and direct service organisations and have challenged the charging out of central services as overheads.

▽　the division between client and contractor leading to organisational changes, which have been particularly marked in shire districts. In some cases radical reviews have departed from the past professional based departments and grouped them around such broad clusters as central services, client services, development services and contract ser-

vices or else split them into small functionally based units or cost centres.

▽   the options given to tenants to opt for another landlord and to schools
to opt out of local authority control have given a stimulus to the growing concern in local authorities for getting close to the customer.

Starting in one service area, these indirect effects have often spread
rapidly into other areas. These changes are leading to the development of a
new pattern of performance management which can involve:

▽   the setting of objectives and targets of managers, who will be given
responsibility for their achievement with a specified level of resources,
which they are allowed to manage free from restrictions upon their use
of those resources

▽   the development and use of performance indicators related to targets
as measures of management performance

▽   accountability for management performance reinforced by systems of
staff appraisal

▽   the development of performance related pay, often associated with
contracts for senior managers.

Occurring widely, these arrangements may involve the creation of units as
accountable cost centres or even trading or quasi-trading arrangements in
which the unit is allowed to charge for its services.

The widest ranging effect of the government's legislation has been its
impact on the culture of the authority or the values and organisational
assumptions underlying its activities. We have seen in Chapter 4 that many
of the existing organisational assumptions have been challenged. In many
cases changes have had a further effect and produced a cultural change as
more overtly commercial values have been adopted or authorities have pursued the aim of the 'Competitive' Council recommended by the Audit
Commission. The pursuit of commercial values or of the model of the
competitive council may not always be based on a full understanding of
commercial practice or of the full implications of competition. There is
however a new language of 'business plans', of 'rewards', of 'contracts' or
of 'trading arrangements'. While this may have its origins in compulsory
competitive tendering it has now attained, in many authorities, a
significance for the organisation as a whole.

Changes supporting local government

Many of these developments can be regarded as achieving the changes
argued for earlier in this book. There is no doubt that the legislative
changes have had effects which are to be welcomed and which can often be
regarded as helping the management of local authorities towards
developing local government. They have, in turn, often been reinforced by
the response to challenges coming from the wider changes already referred
to.

The first, and perhaps the most important, effect has been the challenge to management 'as it happens'. In preparing for compulsory competitive tendering local authorities have had to specify what they required from
a service, rather than rely upon the continuing organisation of the service.

Too often they have found that there were no clear requirements from the service. Responsibility for running the service had enabled the authority to evade the issue of what was required from the service. In the administration of a service, governmental choice can easily be avoided. Authorities have had to work out their requirements from anew. That change has focused the attention of councillors on the choice on what is required rather than on the on-going process of administration.

Once requirements are specified, the local authority has to secure that these requirements are met. Where services were run directly, control was exercised 'as it happened'. If the issue of what is required had not been addressed there was no basis for reviewing whether requirements were met. Compulsory competitive tendering both directly and indirectly focuses attention on inspection and review to secure that requirements are met and at the necessary standard of quality. Indeed CCT has created a new concern for quality, in part because it is recognised that without that concern, quality can suffer in the cost-conscious approach to a contract tightly drawn under commercial pressure. The emphases on monitoring performance and on quality standards have to be seen as advances in management for local government in which both councillors and officers have a role to play. The language and approach demanded for CCT has been seen to have applicability much more widely and has spread rapidly.

The emphasis on the public as customer is not necessarily a direct effect of the legislation, but as was pointed out earlier, the legislation has provided a stimulus to the growing concern for the customer in local authorities. The challenge to a local authority's monopoly, the possibilities for opting out, the introduction of choice in numbers of services have all required the local authority to think more explicitly about their impact on the public. This again can be seen as an important contribution to the changes argued for earlier in this book.

The emphasis on performance management with a focus on objectives and on targets, and on the devolution of management responsibility — with accountability for that responsibility — helps to give direction to the work of the authority as local government. There is also a growing concern for strategic management. Local authorities are reviewing and making explicit their organisational values.

The government's programme has given prominence to the enabling role of the council, although not always in as wide a sense as that described in this book. They have however shown that direct provision is not necessary to the role of local government. In compulsory competitive tendering, the local authority still makes the governmental choice about what is required, even if it no longer undertakes the direct provision of the service. The effect of this change and of arrangements for different services to be provided with or through other agencies has led local authorities to give new consideration to the enabling role. Less emphasis on direct provision has led, in turn, to a recognition of the potential for involvement in the community. The ideas are not new; most local authorities have been concerned with certain key issues for their community. The role, however, has been seen as peripheral rather than central to the life of local authorities and so they have not been organised to pursue it. Now local authorities are considering how they can develop that role as one more central to their purpose.

Generally, then, many of the changes that are taking place in the management of the local authority are in accordance with the directions set out earlier in the book. Many of these changes result from the challenge of the legislation to past patterns of working. Others, however, are the result of initiatives taken within local government, often prompted by other external changes. Both have led authorities to challenge organisational assumptions previously taken for granted and to work towards a new management of local government.

The danger of imbalance

There is another side to the story. The danger of the government's legislation and its effects, both direct and indirect, on the working of local authorities is that it can lead to an imbalance in their working. The need to respond to the demands of the legislation and the consequent single-mindedness of purpose means that there is a danger that some of the aspects of management change argued for earlier in this book are neglected. In particular it can mean neglect of the need for local authorities to be learning organisations, not merely from their own performance, but of problems and issues perceived in the community. It can mean a failure to recognise the political nature of local government and what that means for the role of the councillor. Perhaps most fundamentally it can lead to a neglect of the role of *local government* with the result that the enabling role can be restricted in concept and development.

There are two pressures which lead towards imbalance. First that the government's programme has focused the attention of local authorities more on some aspects of management than others. Thus it has highlighted the role of the contract in the running of the local authority, but it is by no means certain that all organisational or governing relationships can or should be reduced to the terms and conditions of a contract. A contract by its very specificity limits the capacity to adjust and to change in changing circumstances which is at the heart of local government as has been described earlier. A contract is in effect limited to the terms of that contract.

In a certain world in which the tasks to be undertaken can be predetermined, then contracts can define the required relationships. However, local authorities face growing uncertainty in the role of government, enabling their communities to meet changing problems and issues. This requires that they have a high capacity to learn and to adjust to what they have learnt. Local authorities have traditionally (even if imperfectly) learnt through the services they provide. A contract limits that capacity to learn and to adjust.

This is not an argument against the development of contracts, but that contracts are not sufficient by themselves. A local authority needs a capacity beyond the contracts for learning and for change. It is in this sense that there is a danger of imbalance in the development of management. It is not that contracts have no role in the development of the new management, but that a focus on contracts at the expense of other organisational relationships can mean the neglect of important aspects of management for local government.

The second is the pressure to develop a commercial culture, which can be carried to the point where it leads to a neglect of the wider role of local authorities as local government. The Audit Commission has described their model of the effective authority as the *competitive council* and this well illustrates the point that a commercial culture can lead to the pursuit of certain approaches to the management of local authorities at the expense of others. The Audit Commission is right to emphasise that for some purposes a local authority has to be competitive; not least in response to compulsory competitive tendering. The error is to see that as a comprehensive description of the required approach to management.

In the enabling role the local authority could perhaps as well or better be described as the *co-operative council*, working with and through other organisations to meet the needs of the community. The reality is that the local authority needs a plurality of modes of working: it acts as client; it acts as contractor; it acts as enabler; it acts as advocate; it acts as regulator. It is local government.

The danger in adopting a simplistic commercial culture is that while that may be appropriate to competitive activities, a local authority that allows its culture to be wholly dominated by a commercial approach neglects many other aspects of its role. Management in local authorities can learn from management in the private sector and the commercial world just as management there can learn from the world of local government. The mistake is to model the whole of management in local authorities upon the private sector.

There is no one approach to management that can be applied in all circumstances. Research has shown that management in industry varies with the technology. One does not manage a conveyor-belt process in the same way as one manages a research process; equally in local government, the education service is not managed in the same way as the fire service. Management does not vary just with the technology, but also with the purposes, conditions and tasks with which it is concerned. Most important, we need to remember that activities are likely to have been placed in the public sector or in local government to be run in a different way from the private sector. That is not to say that there is an unalienable reason for any particular service to be placed in the public domain, but, once there, there are wider concerns than just commercial transactions.

Local authorities are constituted to consider factors that are not the concern of the private sector. They are concerned with need rather than with demand. The three Es — economy, efficiency and effectiveness — are not a sufficient guide for management in the public domain. There is a fourth E, equity, and a fifth E, environment, for local authorities cannot limit their concerns to their immediate output. They are concerned with the collective needs and interests of their communities. Management in local authorities has to be grounded in the purposes, conditions and tasks of local government.

The danger of the unthinking adoption of a commercial culture is that it can lead to the neglect of these wider considerations. The culture of local authorities needs to be a culture for local government, for that is their role. However, such a culture will be a challenge to past practices, for these tend to be based on professional cultures or cultures of local administration, focusing on continuity of practices. A culture of local government must be outward looking to the community and to the public as customer *and* citizen. It will stress enabling as co-operation with many organisations. It should express a pluralism of aims and a pluralism of methods of provision. It should support the role of the councillor in community leadership. Above all it must express a commitment to local choice and local voice as the medium of community values and to the political processes through which they are expressed.

A commercial culture alone can lead to:

▽ an emphasis on the public as customer, with a neglect for the role of the public as citizen

▽ the management process treated as primary with the political process being regarded as an obstacle rather than an expression of the purposes and conditions of local government

▽ a focus on service alone, without a recognition that local authorities are also as government, ordering, regulating, rationing and choosing as well as providing

▽ a stress on competition, but a neglect of co-operation

▽ the quantitative being pursued at the expense of the qualitative

▽ commercial viability being regarded as the criteria of success, rather than the recognition that in local government many needs have to be balanced and many costs have to be weighed.

Quite simply, the argument must be not that the pursuit of a commercial culture is wrong in itself but that in local government it needs to be balanced by other concerns.

A possible scenario assessed

The result of the emphasis on contracts and the development of the commercial culture could mean that the organisation of local authorities becomes structured as a series of semi-autonomous units which conduct their relationship with each other through contractual or semi-contractual relationships. For example, these could be

▽ contracts made under compulsory competitive tendering between the local authority as contractor and the local authority as client, with a separation into areas of responsibility built into the working of the organisations

▽ contracts made under compulsory competitive tendering between the local authority and a private contractor

▽ contracts developed as a response to the government's legislation on community care

▽ service level agreements made between a central (or indeed part of a service department) department and a service department, specifying the service to be provided by a central department and the cost to be charged for that service, which may be associated with a trading account for the central department

▽ the development of devolved management based on specified targets, with accountability for achievement of those targets and performance related pay, almost represents a semi-contractual agreement.

Going beyond this, the emphasis of much of the remainder of the government's programme, even where not involving contractual or semi-contractual arrangements, is premised on structural separation of different activities:

▽ the regulatory role within social services is to be separated from provision as it is in waste disposal
▽ separate companies have been created to take over responsibilities of local authorities for public transport as in waste disposal
▽ in education, the devolved management of schools means that for many purposes schools will be self-governing and not under the direct control of local authorities, which will have to influence rather than to control
▽ in housing, the ring-fencing of the revenue account could well reinforce the separatism of the housing service.

The cumulative effect of all these changes, some of them the direct effect of legislation, but others a management response guided by the emphasis on contracts and by a commercial culture, has been to heighten the barriers between departments or between units within departments.

There are great strengths in these changes as we have already emphasised. Managers will have greater clarity as to what is required of them; they will have control over the resources required for the achievement of their task; performance will be subject to regular review. The danger lies in the rigidities which this may build into the working of the local authority. The actions of managers will be governed by the terms of the contract, which may be set for a five year period. Service level agreements may both ensure but limit the contribution of the central department. Accountable management, if interpreted as meaning that managers' tasks are defined by the targets set and by those alone, can be a source of rigidity. The more strictly the authority defines the tasks to be performed, the more it limits its capacity to learn and to change. In transforming itself or being transformed into a series of separate units tied for defined periods to specified tasks, the local authority reduces its capacity to respond to change and changing. A structure is being built for certainty, when the 1990s promise the challenge of uncertainty.

In such new rigidities a local authority may lose the capacity for synergy; for the full and flexible use of the local authority's resources, realising the advantages of their being part of a common organisation. It may also lose the capacity to think and act strategically and to produce a corporate response to demands from its environment. Strategic planning and action demands the active participation of the whole and is likely to be limited by fragmentation. Many of the issues facing the local authority do not pay much heed to organisational niceties and discrete boundaries: the environment, the need to develop or conserve, how to meet the demands of relative poverty or relative abundance, or how to relate to the community as a whole demand a corporate response. Few multi-functional commercial organisations would so deny themselves the opportunity for synergy. The ideal of the commercial organisation being adopted may be illusory when contrasted with that reality. Whether it is or not, the local authority must not forget its role as government.

The pre-requisites of local government

If is to be ensured that the local authority retains the potential to develop as local government, certain prerequisites can be identified. First, it has been emphasised that in a changing environment local authorities need *a high capacity for learning*. In the traditional pattern of working, a local authority has learnt through the services provided. That process of learning had its own distortion. It told the local authority more about the problems that it was dealing with than about the opportunities it was not meeting. But the more the activities of a local authority are fragmented into separate units whose boundaries are specified in contractual terms, the more barriers there are to learning. There will be incentives to retain learning in the units to which it belongs. It can be argued that it is improper for client and contractor to share knowledge; heads of direct service organisations have refused to join corporate management teams. Ways need to be found of integrating and devices developed to learn in new ways, for instance, local authorities as clients can develop the inspectoral role, as education authorities are doing and social services departments will be required to. In the development of such a role the need for learning is recognised, but learning must extend beyond the boundaries of existing services. The learning that comes from the councillors' representative role must be used to challenge those boundaries. The centre must ensure a capacity for learning for the authority as a whole.

A local authority needs *a capacity for change*. It requires the flexibility to deal with issues as they arise and for staff to move outside their normal role. Old people's homes, for example, may welcome a cleaner who sees her role as involving more than the specified task. It also requires a capacity to change its activities to meet changing needs. The more the work of the local authority is subject to contractual or semi-contractural agreements, the more difficult it is for the local authority to adapt to changing circumstances, to show flexibility in practice or to respond to political change. Councillors can be trapped within the terms of past contracts. Changes can of course be made when contracts fail to be renewed and contracts can be re-negotiated at a cost. Yet the rigidity introduced by the contract has to an extent been accepted as a fact of life, as has separation in the workings of the local authority which makes it more difficult to combine resources in new ways. While there will be some areas of relative stability where these problems are less likely to arise, the tendency to rigidity must be recognised and every effort made to retain sufficient flexibility.

Local authorities as local government need to recognise *their account-ability to the public as customers and as citizens*. Accountability can and should mean more than the periodic election. It can and should be expressed in an active political process involving both councillors and citizens. It can and should mean an openness for information and a right to explanation. If barriers are built preventing the flow of information and limits are put on explanation then accountability is denied. The tendency for units to be isolated can place limits and build barriers, unless particular effort is made to understand how public accountability can be ensured and the political process be made effective.

And then there is the issue, already mentioned of building, a *culture*

which crosses the internal boundaries and which is supportive of local government.
Where units have their own tasks and their own targets, values that are
inherent in local government — equity, environment, citizenship, community, democracy — can be neglected. Ways have to be found to bring these
basic values into the life of each part of the organisation. A supposedly
commercial culture can thrive on concerns which do not extend beyond the
aims and objectives of particular units; yet if local authorities do not stand
for local government their rationale is lost.

Correcting the balance: the holistic approach re-visited

The main argument of the book, then, has been that a new management of
local authorities is required for the 1990s if local authorities are to realise
their role as local government. It will:

▽   be a different role from that which they had pursued in the post-war
    period which concentrated on the administration of continuing service
    provision on a pre-determined pattern.
▽   encompass the enabling role in its widest sense
▽   be directed at meeting the needs and problems of the community in the
    most effective way, which can include direct provision but does not
    necessarily do so

The basis of the new management required for the role of local authorities
as local government was described in Chapters 2 and 3 and elaborated in
succeeding chapters. It was argued that there is a need to think total and to
adopt an holistic approach; relating different aspects of management to
each other in general management. The developments described in this
chapter show that a new management is being established, but that it may
not fully meet the requirements set out earlier because its origin lies more
in a response to government legislation than in a rounded response to the
wider requirements of the 1990s. There is an imbalance because certain
requirements have been neglected or not been fully met. There has not
been an holistic approach.

Remembering the requirements as set out in Chapter 2 then current
developments:

▽   emphasise closeness to the customer but not to the citizen
▽   neglect or inhibit learning from a changing environment through the
    fragmentation of the authority
▽   have neglected the requirement for effective political process, meaning
    that the role of the councillor as described in Chapter 5 has not been
    adequately developed
▽   can be restrictive if good performance is limited to the achievement of
    pre-determined targets and does not permit space for learning, innova-
    tion and change despite the advantages of devolving responsibility,
    clarifying accountability and reviewing performance
▽   recognise the importance of motivation, but often place a reliance on
    performance related pay rather than emphasising the broader concerns
    of human resource management
▽   mean that there is a primary requirement on the need for strategy and

policy-making in order to set the parameters within which autonomous units can work

▽ highlight the need for organisational values that reflect the nature of local government

▽ mean that there should be an emphasis on the wide variety of relationships possible between the authority and other organisations in the community and not merely contractual relationships recognising that a wide variety of modes of social action are necessary for the full development of the enabling role

▽ demand organisational changes which go beyond the immediate response to legislative change.

The imbalance can be corrected not by abandoning the desirable changes but by complementing them by some of the changes suggested in this book. In addition to

▽ a capacity for learning;
▽ a capacity for change;
▽ accountability to public as customer and citizen;
▽ a culture supportive to local government,

there are three further requirements for the general management of the local authority as local government.

The primacy of the political process

Politics in local government should never be treated as an afterthought. Much worse it should never be treated as an obstacle to good management. It is through politics that the purposes of management are determined and hence the meaning of 'good management' is defined. The changes that are taking place mean that the councillor's role need no longer be focused on the organisation of service provision, but can be focused on the needs and problems faced in the community and on the most effective means of meeting those needs. The councillor's role can become an expression of local government rather than of local administration. This will not just happen, it has to be worked for.

A positive role for the centre and the need for strategy

The more fragmented the organisation of the local authority, the more important is it to rethink and be clear about the role of the centre. This means going beyond what is needed for contract management, where the emphasis is upon the negative of what the centre should no longer do rather than on the positive of what it should do. The role of the centre is to correct the balance. It must stand for a capacity for learning across and beyond the separate units. It must develop a capacity for defining strategy and developing strategic management. It must represent local government.

The emerging need for 'system' management

A new key task that has to be undertaken in the new and complex structure of units each with their own responsibility and with differing relationships with external bodies is 'system' management. System management is the management of the relationships — both internal and external — that structure the working of the authority. It requires organisational and inter-organisational understanding and the capacity to identify imbalance and how that imbalance can be corrected. It is a task for the centre; both of the authority and of departments within it.

The criteria by which one should judge the management of local authorities must be determined by the extent to which it enhances the roles of local government. Despite legislative constraint, local authorities have

▽   a capacity for local choice;
▽   resources of manpower, finance, information and property; and
▽   a wide range of powers to be used for action and influence,

if management can realise them.

The governmental role can however be denied if management is limited to local administration. It is equally denied if management adopts a purely commercial approach. A balance is necessary to support the role of local authorities as local government and that will only be achieved by an holistic approach expressed in general management. That holistic approach can be pursued through the review questions for checking the balance.

Checking the balance: review questions for councillors and officers

▲ Do the workings of departments and committees focus on the public as customer and citizen or on the requirements of the organisation?

▲ Has the authority allowed the boundaries of the organisation to become barriers for the community and for the public?

▲ Does the authority have channels for learning which go beyond the limits of present action and ways of doing things?

▲ Does the authority understand both what its processes for learning tell it and what they do not tell it?

▲ Is the learning, whether from surveys, from dialogue, from suggestion or from complaints actually used?

▲ Has the authority processes for strategic management to balance the necessities of operational management?

▲ Do those processes of strategic management focus choice and give direction?

▲ Does management support and express the political process?

▲ Do the settings and processes of the authority give space for the development both of the representative and the policy and management role?

▲ Does the working of the committee system limit the development of those roles?

▲ What are the organisational values and management style expressed in the workings of the authority?

▲ Are professional values given too much prominence?

▲ Have managers sufficient organisational responsibility for effective resource management and responsiveness in action?

▲ Is the decentralisation of responsibility matched by clarity of policy?

▲ Has the authority the capacity to use the full range of its powers and resources in meeting the needs of the community?

▲ Does the authority understand the resources that lie within the community and which it can work to enhance?

▲ Is performance review built into the workings of departments and committees?

▲ Is performance measured but also assessed and understood?

▲ How seriously does the authority take the management of its human resources?

▲ Does the authority have processes of management and staff develop-
   ment geared to strategic direction?
▲ Are these based on an understanding of the competencies necessary for
   the 1990s?
▲ Is the potential of staff realised in equal opportunities and in communi-
   cation of understanding?
▲ Is organisational innovation constrained by past organisational
   assumptions?
▲ Are organisational assumptions understood in their constraint upon
   change?
And perhaps most important of all,
▲ Is the role of local authorities local administration or local government?
▲ Do the management processes support the role of the local authority as
   local government in enabling the community to meet the needs and
   problems faced?
▲ How far has the local authority developed the general management
   argued for in this book?
From such questions diagnosis can form an agenda for action in correcting
the balance.

Bibliography

Bleakley, W. (1989) *Enabling Authority* Tendring District Council
Bolton Metropolitan District *Extension of Decision Making Practices, Report to Policy Review Sub-Committee*, 28 August 1987
Bradford City Council (1989) *A Model for the 1990s*
Bromley London Borough *The Council's Management Style* (no date)
Cairns, David 'The Local Authority as Lobbyist: the disposal of radioactive waste' *Local Government Policymaking* (December 1987)
Cantle, Ted 'Leicester's Response to the Housing Act' *Local Government Policymaking* (March 1989)
Cheshire County Council (1987) *The Use of County Services in Cheshire*
Clarke, Michael and Stewart, John (1985) *The Public Service Orientation or Does a Public Service Provide a Service for the Public* LGTB
Clarke, M. and Stewart, J. (1988) *Chief Officers: Roles, Dilemmas and Opportunities* LGTB
Clarke, M. and Stewart, J. (1988) *The Enabling Council* LGTB
Clarke, M. and Stewart, J. (1988) *Managing Tomorrow* LGTB
Clarke, M. and Stewart, J. (1989) *Challenging Old Assumptions* LGTB
Clarke, M. and Stewart, J. (1989) *The Councillor and the Enabling Council* LGTB
Clarke, M. and Stewart, J. (1990) *Developing Effective Public Service Management* LGTB
Clarke, M. and Stewart, J. *Effective Public Service Management* LGTB
Cooke, Arthur 'Conflicting Interests', *Public Finance and Accountancy*, 9 June 1989
Cumbria County Council (1989) *A statement from the Group Leaders to all employees*
Enfield London Borough (1989) *Corporate Identity Launch*
Gallant, Victor 'Developing a strategic response to unemployment' *Local Government Policymaking*, 1 June 1988
Geeson, Tony and Haward, John 'Devolved Management — The Berkshire Experience' *Local Government Studies* (January/February 1990)
Hackney London Borough *Quality of Service Review 1989/90: Report to the Policy and Resources Committee* 5 September 1989
Hancox, Andy; Worall, Les and Page, John, 'Developing a Customer Orientated Approach to Service Delivery: the Wrekin Approach' *Local Government Studies* (January/February 1989)
Harlow District Council (1989) *Citizens Charter*
Hoggett, Paul and Hambleton, Robin (1985) *Decentralisation in Birmingham, Report to ESRC*
Kirklees Metropolitan Council and Friends of the Earth (1989) *Kirklees State of the Environment Report*

Latham, Don (1989) *Avon's Revitalised Performance Review and Decision Making Process*

Lincolnshire County Council (3 November 1989) *Organisation and Structure of Lincolnshire County Council, Report of the Chief Executive to the Policy and Resources Committee*

Local Government Training Board *Blyth Valley District Council: Management and Organisation Development and Member Participation*

Local Government Training Board (1986) *Survey of Public Attitudes*

Local Government Training Board (1987) *Getting Closer to the Public*

Local Government Training Board (1988) *Going for Better Management*

Local Government Training Board (1988) *Learning From the Public*

Local Government Training Board (1989) *Trends in New Management*

Middlesbrough Borough Council (1989) *Policy in Action*

Murray, Nicholas 'A Service Business', *Local Government Chronicle* (18 August 1989)

Normann, Richard (1989) *Service Management*, John Wiley

Northamptonshire County Council *Newsletter of the Central Services Review*

Reading Borough Council (1988) *Why a Strategy*

Rochdale Metropolitan District (1989) *Policies for the 1990s*

Sabin, Paul, 'The Role of the Chief Executive and the Management of County Councils' in Ken Young (ed) *New Directions for County Government* Association of County Councils and INLOGOV (1989)

Scampion, John, 'Public Service in Practice' *Local Government Studies* (May/June 1988)

Stewart, John and Stoker, Gerry, 'The "Free Local Government" Experiments and the programme of Public Service Reform in Scandinavia' in Colin Crouch and David Marquand (1989) *The New Centralism* Basil Blackwell

The Widdicombe Committee of Inquiry into the Conduct of Local Authority Business (1986) Research Volume 1, *The Political Organisation of Local Authorities*, Cmnd 1798, HMSO

Wiltshire County Council June 1988 *Development of a Rural Strategy for Wiltshire, Report to the Policy and Resources Committee*

York City Council (1989) *Customer Contracts and Audits*

Index